PLEASURES AND TREASURES

MODEL RAILWAY ENGINES

J. E. MINNS

MODEL RAILWAY ENGINES

G. P. PUTNAM'S SONS
NEW YORK

Acknowledgements

The photographs in this book are reproduced by kind permission of the following: G. Barlow: 94, 97, 98, 99, 100, 101, 106, 108, 109; Andrew Bruce: 3, 7, 9, 14, 15, 19, 20, 26, 29, 31, 34, 39, 40, 42, 44, 47, 49, 50, 51, 52, 53, 54, 55, 56, 57, 58, 59, 60, 61, 62, 64, 65, 66, 67, 68, 69, 70, 71, 72, 73, 74, 75, 76, 77, 78, 79, 80, 81, 82, 84, 85, 86, 87, 88, 89, 90, 96, 104, 105, 119; Robin Butterell: 46, 91, 103, 113; Christie's: 1, 33, 38, 45, 63; N. F. Du Pille: 38; R. Hines: 118; E. J. Howlett: 7; Irish Collection: 3, 14, 15, 19, 26, 34, 39, 40, 44, 51, 55, 68, 69, 70, 90, 104, 105; W. H. McAlpine: 43, 86; A. Plumb: 119; private collections: 1, 33, 36, 45, 53, 56, 59, 63, 71, 74, 75, 76, 77, 78, 79, 80, 81, 85, 88, 89, 91, 92, 93, 94, 95, 106, 107, 108, 109, 113, 118; Richard C. Rapier (*Remunerative Railways*): 48; Edward Reeves: 24; The Science Museum, London: 4, 5, 6, 8, 10, 11, 12, 13, 16, 17, 18, 20, 21, 22, 23, 27, 28, 29, 30, 32, 35, 36, 37, 41, 47, 110, 111, 112, 114, 115, 116, 117; Deutsches Museum, Munich: 46; J. Southern: 2, 120; E. A. Steele: 92, 93, 95, 102, 107. From the author's collection: 9, 24, 25, 31, 48, 49, 50, 52, 54, 57, 58, 60, 61, 62, 64, 65, 66, 67, 82, 84, 87.

The author would also like to thank the following people for their help and patience during the preparation of this book: G. Barlow, R. Butterell, W. E. Finlayson, R.S. Guinness, E. J. Howlett, E. H. McAlpine, E. A. Steele and Mrs E. A. Steele and J. T. Van Riemsdijk of the Science Museum, London.

ENDPAPERS: One of the most fascinating nineteenth-century miniature railway locomotives, the *Pioneer*, built in 1873-4 by Richard C. Rapier for the Woosung Railroad on the banks of the Yangtse River, China.

Contents

Introduction

The history of the steam locomotive stretches from the late eighteenth century to roughly the middle of the twentieth. At a time when practical space travel is a normality, it is already fantastic to look back on machines so incredibly crude in conception. In fifty years, people will be trying to explain to their incredulous children that for a century and a half men rushed about filling metal contained on wheels with water, lit a fire underneath, waited an hour and a half for steam to be produced and then careered off at speeds in excess of a hundred mph-with smoke, steam and cinders flying out of a hole in the front of the machine, totally obscuring their line of vision.

Crude though they were, and never reaching an overall efficiency of more than nine and a half per cent, steam locomotives, like no other method of transport, continued to captivate and absorb designers, employees and enthusiasts. At all stages of development they were larger than life, almost living, machines, presenting an image of great power and beauty. Since railways affected social conditions, politics and business it is little wonder that men have spent millions of hours making both working and non-working models of their favourite locomotive prototypes.

At first, it was cheaper and safer to make these models purely and simply to test an idea. Then one went on to the full-size engine from the model. Today this is normal practice with ships, aircraft, car bodies, space craft and so on. In those days it was

1 (*opposite*) A 5-in gauge model of Hackworth's Stockton and Darlington Railway 2-2-2 locomotive No. 24, *Magnet*, of 1838, built by R. Ockleford in 1850. It is hotbar-fired, and fitted with slip-eccentric reversing, leather-covered spring buffers and lever-type safety-valves.

entirely new, and marked the beginning of the science of industrial development modelling.

As time went on, and the early developmental stages (between the 1780s and the 1820s) passed into the period of the widespread growth of railways (between 1830 and 1860), models were made by locomotive companies and professional instrument-makers as trophies and for sales promotion exhibition purposes. The skill necessary to make such complex and accurate pieces of miniature machinery, was still a rarity, and few private or amateur engineers built models.

Between the 1860s and the 1890s amateur enthusiasts everywhere began building models, and, recognising the popularity of the subject, hundreds of toy manufacturers all over the world began to turn out steam, clockwork and hand-pushed models of the earlier locomotives. Earlier, locomotives had been produced perhaps because people recognised the commercial value of pandering to sentiment or to the nostalgia of a middle-aged director longing for the old long-funnelled locomotives of his youth; certainly it remains a fair generalisation to say that during that period commercial models represented prototypes of up to thirty years old.

Electrically-powered models soon became available, and the great period between the 1890s and the 1930s of vast and yet more vast and elaborate layouts began engulfing otherwise totally sane households all over the world. This period also encompassed enthusiasts with the time, land, madness and money to create brilliantly complex miniature railways with locomotives weighing as much as a ton and a half, and capable of pulling a hundred passengers at the slightest excuse, whether they liked it or not.

Thus it is that locomotive models fall into five categories, namely those built for development purposes; for exhibition or patent purposes; amateur or 'scratch' built models; commercially available brass, cast-iron or tinplate, steam, clockwork and electric toys; and miniature or large-gauge models. At all levels of likeness and quality, they survive where their prototypes have long since been destroyed, in some cases passing on a wealth of information about the past and in others simply preserving the sculptural beauty inherent in locomotive design, or the personality of the builder.

Locomotives are described or grouped by their wheel arrangements. Whereas one talks in terms of tonnage with shipping, thrust in aviation and so on, a locomotive with four wheels, that is to say two leading, two driving and no trailing, is termed a 2-2-0; a large American articulated locomotive which might have four leading, eight driving and no trailing wheels on the leading frame, and the same but the opposite way round on the trailing frame, is termed a 4-8-8-4 locomotive. These wheel arrangements were further categorised into classes, the most famous of which were the 4-4-2 'Atlantic' and the 4-6-2, 'Pacific'.

Most locomotives consist basically of a horizontal boiler with a firebox at the driving end and a smokebox and chimney at the other, supported on two or more frames to which cylinders are fixed. The cylinders drive the wheels round by a system of long jointed connecting-rods attached to either their axle or to a spoke. In this book a series of contemporary models has been used to illustrate briefly the historical development and to pay a small tribute to one of the greatest modelling stories in history.

It must be added, in conclusion, that any steam-driven machinery has utterly personal and readily recognisable characteristics, both good and bad. Locomotive drivers used to say that even with two identical designs of locomotive, built consecutively, each would behave quite differently under steam, and the man and his engine had to work as one. This is also the case with models – each having its own good and bad moods – some would say even opinions! One man, after spending three and half years building his engine, was seen to have such a furious argument with it when getting to know it under steam that he never spoke to it again and got to know his wife instead.

2 A really magnificent $7\frac{1}{4}$-in gauge model of the London Midland and Scottish Railway 'Pacific' locomotive and tender No. 6230, *Duchess of Buccleuch*, which is exceedingly accurate and to scale, and runs beautifully. It is one of H. C. Powell's finest creations, and not untypical of the current standards achieved by both amateur and professional builders. 21ins high by 112ins long.

CHAPTER ONE

The Early Years

SINCE civilisation began, man has shown a longing to spend time and patience recreating in miniature the objects surrounding his life. The challenge of the necessary intricacy and skill coupled with the artistic satisfaction achieved have left us countless examples of this form of self-expression. These objects have played an important part in attempts to analyse the individual lives and customs of the races who produced them, and have handed down vital information to archaeologists, scientists and sociologists.

As technology advanced, a new use for modelling appeared, since it was so much easier and less expensive to build a working model of a theory than risk life and limb with full-size machine or apparatus. Early textbooks are full of illustrations of models depicting highly ingenious but sometimes rather terrifying inventions.

When in 1763 James Watt, an instrument-maker in Glasgow University, was asked to repair a demonstration model of a Newcomen engine, one of the first practical forms of steam power, he quickly discovered its inefficiencies, and, having a strongly analytical mind, set about rectifying the design by making a model of a separate condenser—an invention which paved the way to his incredible career and the beginnings of practical power for industry.

Watt, with Matthew Boulton, at the Soho Iron Works in Birmingham, concentrated his energies on improving industrial power. At a very early period he was proposing to apply his own

4 A conjectural model of Trevithick's locomotive *Catch-Me-Who-Can* which ran in London in 1808. Note the feed-pump driven through a lever off the crosshead, and the exhaust steam feed-water heater.

3 (*opposite*) Trevithick's much improved third 4¾-in gauge model of 1797, with its internal regulator, lever-type safety-valve, shaped connecting-rods and plug-valve gear. The front axle is pivoted for steering. 13½ins high by 9ins long.

5 A reproduction of William Murdoch's model locomotive of 1784; the model had a flue boiler and a single vertical cylinder, ¾-in bore by 2-in stroke, connected to 9½-in driving wheels through a grasshopper beam. 14ins high by 19¼ ins long.

engine to locomotion, using either a non-condensing design that derived no help from the partial vacuum caused when steam is turned back into water in a cooling vessel or an air-surface condenser under the radiator; in fact he actually included a design in his patent of 1784. But it was his assistant, William Murdoch, who in the same year made the first working model locomotive [figure 5]. This model was said to run from 6 to 8 miles an hour, its driving wheels making from 200 to 275 rpm, a speed which must have terrified contemporary engineers and laymen, alike. Indeed, when it was run one night in a dark avenue leading to the Redruth church, and was encountered by the parson, the poor man was frightened out of his wits. Murdoch was then still under the employ of James Watt and Matthew Boulton, as their Cornish representative, and he was immediately threatened with dismissal by Watt if he continued to experiment along those lines.

The added risk of an even worse diplomatic breakdown in relations between Cornwall and Birmingham was Watt's reason for this threat. The severe patent levies imposed on the Cornishmen for the use of Watt pumping engines had caused a lot of friction and antagonism. The Cornish, however, had amongst their ranks a young, impetuous and highly inventive champion by the name of Richard Trevithick, born in 1771. It was soon realised that his enormous physical strength was well matched by an incredible ability to churn out numerous hurriedly-conceived ideas, which he would often convey in his semi-illiterate way to his great friend, Davis Giddy, whom he had met in London during one of the battles with Boulton and Watt over patent infringements. In trying to improve the steam-engines under his charge in the many mines of Cornwall, he decided to try 'strong steam', which meant steam at about 30 psi and above; this would obviate the necessity of using a separate condenser and allow the machinery and boiler to be much smaller. These experiments proved a great success, and it was not long after Murdoch's experimental steam-locomotive that Trevithick embarked upon a series of three models to demonstrate his theory that, by merely adding wheels, these comparatively small 'portable' steam engines could travel under their own power to the head of a new mineshaft, be jacked up, and set to work as flexible little high-speed winding engines. Of the three models, only two remain; Francis Trevithick, his son, later talked of the first being demonstrated on the kitchen table in about 1796, and it is thought that the others were made in 1797.

Trevithick's second model [figure 6], now preserved at the Science Museum in London, is similar to Murdoch's in basic design, but nevertheless shows some distinct improvements. The general workmanship is simple, but good where it has to be, no effort whatsoever having been made to embellish a piece of practical enthusiasm with decorated working. It was left at the works of Whitehead and Co. of Manchester, who were manufacturing engines for him in 1804.

In what is considered to be his third model [figure 3], the workmanship is better and the beginnings of simple engineering decorations are evident. Once again the model has no chimney, but, unlike the three-wheel engine which was fired by hot iron, this model has a rudimentary Cornish boiler and was fired by hot coals placed in a tray, the gases of which escaped through the seven holes along both sides of the boiler-barrel.

When finished and tested on Christmas Eve 1801, the full-size Camborne road locomotive, which followed the general design of the three-wheel engine, was set off on a celebration trip to meet Davis Giddy. Unfortunately the front wheel hit a stone on the road, wrenching the steering-tiller from his great friend Captain Vivian's hands, and all and sundry careened into the nearest ditch. This in itself was not so grave a thing, since ready help was available to right the engine and coax it into the nearest shed. Sadly, however, the accident happened just outside a fine public house, noted for its good roast goose and excellent ale, and the party adjourned for sustenance. They became so engrossed that they forgot the water-level in the boiler and within minutes little was left of either engine or shed: The model and the steam carriage did, however, result in the 1802 patenting of high-pressure engines by Trevithick and Vivian.

It can be assumed that Trevithick built *Catch me who Can* [fig-

6 Trevithick's second model of 1796. Though similar to Murdoch's model, the hand-beaten copper boiler with its comparatively large heating area, and the vertical cylinder 1.55-in bore by 3.4-in stroke set into it, are much more sophisticated. Steam is controlled in the double-acting cylinder through a semi-rotary plug-valve, actuated by a vertical crosshead, mounted, slotted plug-rod. Small screw-jacks are fitted to the underside of the main driving-wheel bearings so that the engine could be lifted, thus converting it into a stationary engine.

ure 4] from this third model. The locomotive ran for a short time in 1808 on a circular railway in London. In a way this model has more significance, since it subsequently found its way to an instrument shop to be purchased in 1811 by Francisco Uville, who found it whilst searching for steam-engines with which to drain the Peruvian mines. He paid twenty guineas for it, carried it to Lima, and lost no time in successfully trying it on the highest ridges of Pasco. In 1812 Uville returned, landed at Falmouth and found its inventor, and as a result Trevithick sailed for Peru in 1816. After quite incredible adventures he returned to England in 1827, having left others to reap the benefits of his pioneering work in the field of locomotive design. He died in poverty in 1833 at the age of sixty-two.

The famous Pen-y-Darran locomotive of 1804 [figure 7] was built by Trevithick to win a wager for five hundred guineas. It was the first railway-locomotive in the world, and although this model is faithfully copied from the drawings handed down, it is as incomplete as they, and remains only as a guide to its historic prototype.

A Trevithick engine was ordered by Christopher Blackett of the Wylam Colliery, and, although it was never used, he was determined to try steam-haulage on his plateway. His foreman of the smiths was Timothy Hackworth (1786-1850) and his colliery viewer was William Hedley. It was Hedley who in 1811 built a model [figure 8] to demonstrate adhesion, consisting of a wooden frame with four wheels coupled by spur-wheels which in turn were driven by outside hand-cranks. The experiment was a success, and in 1813 a single-cylinder engine with cast-iron boiler, single internal flue and large flywheel was constructed. It was not, of course, successful, and another, with wrought-iron boiler, return-flue and twin outside cylinders was constructed by Hackworth—the famous *Puffing Billy*.

The progress of Hedley and Hackworth had been watched by George Stephenson, who built his first engine, *Blucher*, in 1814, and his Killingworth engine [figure 11] in 1815. Slowly Stephenson's fame spread, and after more developments and designs he

became confident of the advantages of rail transport over that offered by the canals. The Hetton Railway was opened in 1822, and some five Stephenson improved Killingworth locomotives were set to work. So began commercial railways, and with it the competitive nature of steam-locomotive designers that lasted until the end of the great steam-locomotive era.

7 A conjectural 4¾-in gauge model of Trevithick's Pen-y-Darran and Wylam locomotive , built by W. Mason who also built the equivalent models at the Science Museum, London and at Cairo. The feed-pump and feed-water heater have been left out owing to their omission on contemporary artists' drawings. Note the return-flue boiler. 10½ins high by 17ins long.

8 Hedley's 8¼-in gauge model of 1811, built to demonstrate the traction possible with smooth cast-iron wheels which can be moved by the cranks and inter-connecting spur wheels. 21½ins long.

9 (*opposite*) Timothy Hackworth's little known 4¼-in gauge model 0-4-0 locomotive. It is the original design of the *Sans Pareil* of 1826. Here one can see how closely Hackworth and Stephenson worked. The vertical semi-immersed cylinders and valve arrangement are typical of Stephenson's Killingworth engines, whilst the method of connecting is reminiscent of Hedley's model. It is hot-coals-fired. 13½ins high by 9½ ins long.

Stephenson, recognising the potential competition, tried to employ Hackworth at the locomotive works, and finally secured him as general manager of the Stockton and Darlington Railway, for which *Locomotion* [figure 10] was built at the works of R. Stephenson & Co., Newcastle-on-Tyne, in 1825.

Engineers, as such, were extremely rare and sought-after men. Before, there was almost no category between on the one hand blacksmiths of varying skill, and, on the other, clock- and instrument-makers and gunsmiths. So it was, then, that many of the development, patent and exhibition models that have taught us so much about their designers were in fact made by instrument-makers used to working on small machinery to high degrees of finish and accuracy.

Figure 9 is a most interesting example of coordination between Hackworth and a local clock-maker. The model is undoubtedly Hackworth's, having a label on the inside of the box describing it as his *Sans Pareil* – a design, for the prize of five hundred guineas, for the best engine on the Manchester and Liverpool Railway. The gears, however, are without doubt the work of a clock-maker as is the flywheel, and the four turned brass pillars supporting the boiler off the cast-brass frame are typical of the pillars used to separate the motion-plates in a grandfather clock. This is also the first engine model known to the writer which shows conscious decoration, namely the knops on the connection-rods.

In 1827 Hackworth built the *Royal George No. 5* [figure 12], a design for coal traffic on the Stockton and Darlington Railway.

16

10 (*above*) A 7¼-in gauge model of Robert
Stephenson's Stockton and Darlington Railway
0-4-0 locomotive and tender No. 1, *Locomotion*,
of 1825, by T.A. Common. Here, connecting-
rods have begun, and highly elaborate parallel
motion is fitted. A seat is fitted above the running
board. 20¼ins high by 35¾ins long.

11 (*above right*) A 7-in gauge model of George
Stephenson's Killingworth 0-4-0 locomotive and
tender of 1815, built by Twining. It follows
Trevithick's practice of semi-internally-mounted
cylinders. Slide-valves are used and the engine
was driven from the running boards. Note the
chain wheel coupling device. 28ins high and
38½ins long.

12 (*right*) Timothy Hackworth's 3½-in gauge
model 0-6-0 locomotive, *Royal George No.* 5 of
1827, built for the Stockton and Darlington
railway. Here he has used inverted grasshopper
beams to obtain parallel motion and valve
movement, but the equalised sprung axles,
connecting-rods and cast-iron frame are also
significant improvements. 13¼ins high by 13ins
long.

13 Stephenson's 3¾-in gauge model of 1828, probably sent to Edinburgh for demonstration. It is hot-iron-fired, and has flangeless wheels with axles running in solid bearings. The cylinders are now, after Hackworth practice, outside the boiler, but four connecting-rods are still retained despite the coupling-rod. There is an interesting system of valve driving motion between the frames, which causes the engine to go backwards and forwards automatically for a few feet. 14ins high by 10½ins long.

Overleaf
14 A beautiful contemporary 4¾-in gauge instrument-maker's model of Stephenson's 2-2-0 *Planet*-type locomotive and tender of the Liverpool and Manchester Railway of 1831. The engine had outside frames, inside cylinders placed in the smokebox, steam-dome and water-jacketed firebox integrally made with the tubular boiler. The cranked axle and driving-wheels were nearest to the firebox. The model has correct valve-gear, finely decorated chimney, tender frames and wheel spokes. All the handles that get hot are ivory, and it carries a large-capacity spirit-tank with burner for the internally-fired tubular boiler. Two feed-pumps are driven off the main axle and the springs and frames are above the axles. 12ins high by 27ins long.

15 D. Erskine's 3⅝-in gauge patent/sales model 2-2-0 locomotive of 1833. It was hot-bar-fired and had a whistle and waterlevel test-cocks fitted to the boiler. It was also fitted with most interesting, if impractical, valve-gear. Eccentric-operated plug-valves are placed on the outside of the smokebox, and mounted inside cylinders, and the ports are piped up into a 'reversing box' with a slide-valve inside, mounted on the side of the smokebox and controlled by a reach-rod from the footplate. 8ins high by 8½ins long.

The model was built to demonstrate to the directors the sound-ness of his ideas, and includes many interesting features. Stephen-son seems to have been somewhat influenced by this design, as his model of 1828 [figure 13] shows.

Up until this time, the only passenger-coach in service on the Stockton and Darlington Railway was *Experiment* [figure 16], built in 1826 to carry six inside passengers and a further wind-blown, soot-covered fifteen outside. Demand for the new fast transport showed every sign of increasing, and profitability fig-ures were already far surpassing those of canal economics. Thus it was that in 1829 the directors of the Liverpool and Manchester Railway offered a prize of £500 for the most efficient locomotive. Amongst the stipulations was that the said engine must effectively consume its own smoke, according to the provisions of the Rail-way Act, 7, George IV. The entries were Braithwaite and Erics-son's *Novelty*, Timothy Hackworth's *Sans Pareil*, Robert Stephen-son's *Rocket*, Burstall's *Perseverance* and Brandreth's *Cycloped*, these last two being unsatisfactory.

When the *Novelty* (figure 17) was first tried, the wheels were found to be wrong, and Hackworth himself did the necessary modifications, but the engine finally had to be withdrawn. Hack-

16 A contemporary 9½-in gauge model of the Stockton and Darlington Railway coach of 1826 which, although first-class, is unsprung. 14ins high by 10½ins long.

17 (*opposite left*) A 7-in gauge model of Ericson's 0-4-0 *Novelty* of the Rainhill trials of 1829, with its two table engines and internal coupling rods. 13½ins high by 19½ins long.

18 (*opposite right*) A 7¼-in gauge model of the Liverpool and Manchester Railway first-class coach, *Experience*, of 1834, with its sprung axles and buffers, and traditional coachman's seats on the roof. 15¼ins high by 29½ins long.

worth's *Sans Pareil* was next. He had had the cylinders made at the works of R. Stephenson, and six were made before two perfect ones could be fitted. During the trial, one of the cylinders burst and was then found to be only $\frac{1}{16}$ in thick!—smart man Stephenson. The exhaust was blasted up the chimney, and in fact the *Sans Pareil* was faster, more powerful and consumed less coke than the *Rocket*, and continued in service elsewhere, practically without alteration until 1844. Stephenson was quick to realise the difference in draught up the chimney and calmly asked Hackworth, 'Timothy, what makes the sparks fly out of the chimney?' to which Hackworth replied, 'It is the end of this little fellow that does the business.' He was referring to the nozzle which caused the exhaust steam to blast up the chimney; that night, men entered the engine-house, opened the smokebox and in the morning the *Rocket* was altered; it went on to win the prize, being the only engine left in the race. Apart from all this splendid libel, the most significant thing about the *Rocket* was that it had a multi-fire-tube boiler (in which fire tubes conveyed the flames and smoke through the boiler) which greatly increased the heating surface, and although the firebox was, as it were, separate, fire tubes were to be standard practice from then on.

After various other improvements, Stephenson & Co. produced what can be considered the first locomotive to set a principle of design thought which was maintained until the last locomotives built. This engine was called the *Planet*; figure 14 is a beautiful example of a sales model made in about 1831. It is clearly a working one and was almost certainly used for sales demonstration and exhibition. Once again it is the work of an instrument-maker, and is initialled in the same way as contemporary scientific aparatus.

The reversing system on the *Planet*-type locomotives was difficult to operate and many attempts were made to design alternative systems. The little silver-plated 2-2-0 (i.e. two front, two driving and no trailing wheels) locomotive model [figure 15] must surely have been an attempt to try out and sell an alternative

design in about 1833. Made by D. Erskine of Edinburgh, the model is only 8 ins long, and was probably designed to be readily transportable for demonstrations.

The 1830s saw the development of a whole series of new locomotive building companies—Hawthorn & Co.; Roberts of the firm Sharp, Roberts & Co.; George Forrester & Co.; Vauxhall Foundry, Liverpool; Tayleur & Co.; Bury & Co. of Liverpool; Stirling & Co. and J. and C. Carmichael of Dundee—to name but a few. By and large, designs tended to become more and more standard. Only a few relatively odd designs were tried and abandoned. Amongst them was the amazing Roberts *Experiment* class 2-2-0, brought out in 1833.

These extraordinary locomotives had vertical cylinders mounted on the running boards just behind the smokebox, with bell-cranks bringing the motion to the driving wheels. The valves were a form of piston-valve, and were worked directly off the bell-crank of the opposite cylinder. Four were built, one for the Liverpool and Manchester Railway and the other three for the Dublin and Kingstown Railway. It is also worthy of note that R. Stephenson & Co. constructed a locomotive for the Saratoga and Schenectady Rail Road of America in that year. Owing to the short curves, it was fitted with a leading pivoted carriage or 'bogie', so called because the low wagons used on the quarries at Newcastle were locally called 'bogies'. The *Experiment*-type 2-2-0 locomotives supplied to the Dublin Kingstown Railway were not

Overleaf

19 A magnificent contemporary $6\frac{1}{2}$-in gauge model of the Dublin and Kingstown Railway type 2-2-0 Forrester and Co. locomotive No. 51, *Colossus*, of 1834, which was probably built for exhibition purposes. It is fitted with two feed-pumps on top of the frames which are driven through rockers worked off the crossheads, a screw-operated hand-brake acting on one side of the tender, and a pioneering four-eccentric gab-valve gear. The smokebox tubeplate is covered by a set of louvred shutters for damping, controlled from the cab, and the buffers are not of the leather-sheathed coil-spring type, but bear on leaf-springs mounted across the frames front and back. 18ins high by 45ins long.

20 A fine $5\frac{1}{8}$-in gauge model of a London and Southampton Railway 2-2-2 locomotive of 1837. It is fitted with four-eccentric gab-valve gear, the gabs being supported from links suspended from the footplate-controlled reversing – or weight-shaft. The base of each gab can be brought to engage with pins on the valve push-rods, the span of the gabs being equal to the valve travel. They can also be totally disengaged so as to allow independent hand movement by means of the two levers visible on the footplate. It has a haystack boiler with a circular firebox. $14\frac{1}{4}$ins high by $18\frac{3}{4}$ins long.

a success, and they then ordered three Forrester 2-2-0 tender engines similar to *Colossus* [figure 19]. This model is one of the finest early examples ever seen by the author. The high quality, combined with careful choice of materials, makes a lasting impression. It is possible that the model was sent down for sales purposes to the directors of the London and Greenwich Railway which was opened in 1836, since the tender bears a composite coat of arms, the second and third quarters of which were intended to be those of the city of London. In point of fact, that railway never purchased a Forrester tender engine, despite the water-colour of a similar tender engine painted in the same livery which was in their offices. They did, however, purchase tank-engines of the 2-2-0 type.

During the growth in the number of locomotive builders, the world as a whole started to accept rail transport as vital for industrial, political and social advance, and railway companies started up everywhere. The District Superintendent of the London and Southampton Railway, J. Dawson, built the beautiful 2-2-2 brass model [figure 20] in 1837. It is excellently finished, but, as is so frequently found in models of recent times, compromises such as a solid frame and spring castings were used. This engine was privately built, but many of the finer examples of the nineteenth century, as already discussed, were professionally built, and the degree of accuracy depended, as always, on price and time. Figure 1 is another good contemporary example, and the level of comfort offered passengers at that time is exemplified by the models in figures 21 and 23.

21 (*left*) A 7¼-in gauge model of a Bodmin and Wadebridge second-class carriage of 1837, showing generally cruder construction typical of lesser railway companies. 14ins high by 18ins long.

22 (*right*) A 7¼-in gauge model of a Lancashire and Yorkshire Railway second-class carriage of 1839. Here, better coach work is apparent, and the original was used on the Manchester and Leeds Railway. 15ins high by 25½ins long.

23 (*opposite below*) A 7¼-in gauge model showing the blowy existence of passengers travelling third-class on the Bodmin and Wadebridge Railway in 1840. 8ins high by 24ins long.

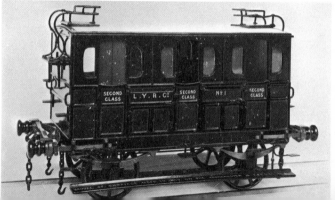

Figure 24 is a contemporary 5¼ in gauge Stephenson 2-2-2 of the same period. The frames, cylinder arrangement and valve-gear are much the same as those in figure 20, but the boiler is fundamentally Stephenson with the square firebox of the enlarged type. The engine has obviously worked a good deal, since not only are the firebars distorted and coloured but the engine, when recently steamed, performed excellently with a very sharp cut-off and evenly timed 'beat'. Its maker, A. C. Hedges, was an instrument-maker and once again solid brass frames and springs were used. It has been suggested that it was probably a South Eastern Railway locomotive. Edward Bury, a competent rival designer and builder, had given Robert Stephenson many ideas, ideas which resulted originally in the *Planet* having horizontal inside-cylinders and a cranked axle, but the model of Bury's 2-2-2 *Comet* [figure 29] represents possibly one of his most successful designs. The model is complete with wonderful scale-size fittings, frame and motion details, and the horse-shoe tender has cast side-frames with diamond designs which had already become traditional.

The middle of the 1830s saw the foundation of the Great Western Railway under the guiding hands of Brunel, Wood and Hawkshaw. The first locomotives were ordered in 1836 from the Vulcan Foundry; Mather, Dixon & Co., Liverpool; Hawthorn & Co., Newcastle; the Haigh Foundry Co. and R. Stephenson & Co. Daniel Gooch (later Sir Daniel Gooch) started work as locomotive superintendent in August 1837, having served under Stephenson at the Vulcan Foundry. Not all the engines finally delivered were satisfactory, but in the January 1838 trials it was

24 A 5¼-in gauge model of a South Eastern Railway 2-2-2 locomotive of 1840, built by A.C. Hedges about 1850, with proper boiler, gab-valve gear and simulated springs. Note the fluted steam dome. 16ins high by 20ins long.

25 This shows motion details of the same locomotive; notice the upward-looking forks or gabs, in the bottom of which ride the levers which come up to control the valves above the cylinders, piston, crosshead and guide bars, inside frames, weight shaft, reversing reach-rod and lever.

Overleaf
26 A beautiful 5¼-in gauge model of the Hawthorn Edinburgh and Glasgow Railway 0-4-2 locomotive and tender, *Vulcan*, and five wagons of 1842, so typical of a full-size train of the period. It was built as a working model although there are no feed-pumps fitted.

found that the broad-gauge lines were in fact, so beautifully firm, smooth, and true, that the engines glided over them more like a shuttle through a loom or an arrow out of a bow than like the effect on any previous railway'. As time passed Sir Daniel Gooch came to find that he could rely only on the engines from the Vulcan Foundry with the exception of Stephenson's *North Star*, and so it was that his ability to design good locomotives manifested itself in the fine 2-2-2 locomotive in figure 27. This model, with its beautifully constructed mahogany-lagged haystack boiler, was made for exhibition and later presented to Sir Daniel. It represents his famous 'Ixion' class and has on it some wonderful detail work.

As with all works of art, the style of the individual varies enormously, and often a comparatively crude example has tremendous charm and character. Figure 26 shows a 5¼ in gauge model of a Hawthorn 0-4-2 locomotive and tender of about 1842. *Vulcan* and her train of two first-class carriages, a second-class carriage,

27 A really beautiful 10½-in gauge contemporary model of a Great Western Railway Gooch 2-2-2 'Ixion' class broad-gauge locomotive and tender of 1840, with its outside fletched frames, working springs, gab-valve gear and typical mahogany-lagged haystack boiler. Note the brake gear and tool boxes on the tender. 22¾ins high by 58¾ins long.

28 The under-frame of 'Ixion', showing the beautiful shaping in workmanship so typical of nineteenth-century design and practice. The rods from top to bottom are forward eccentric rod and gab; crosshead-driven feed-pump and plunger; connecting- and piston-rods; inside frame; reverse eccentric push-rod and gab; second cylinder connecting piston-rods and so on. Note the bottom of the firebox with its visible stay-heads on the left, and the four sets of crosshead guide-bars on the right.

a livestock waggon and a brake/guards van is 11 ft 6 ins long. It must have been made by an enthusiast to run, since all the fittings, for practical reasons, are built oversize. At some time it must have changed hands, and the gab valve-gear was modified by its new owner to conform to the more modern and efficient Stephenson's link motion ingeniously added over the gabs. Crudity can be seen here in the choice of materials and the use of simplified techniques and ideas such as the square nuts on the smokebox front plate, the 'oven' door latch on the smokebox door, and the wooden side-frames of the horse-shoe type tender. The carriages are all soldered tinplate painted in various liveries, some as found with the engine and others as found later, but the paint is original and gives a very good idea of what a train of that period must have looked like.

At this time, speeds of one hundred miles an hour were feasible. It is interesting that only twenty years before the following exchange took place between Stephenson and a committee of the House of Commons: 'Suppose, now, one of your engines to be going at the rate of 9 or 10 miles an hour, and that a cow were to stray upon the line and get in the way of the engine, would not that be a very awkward circumstance?', to which he replied, 'Yes, very awkward—for the cow!'

In fact, as early as 1812 in America, Colonel John Stevens predicted speeds of up to 100 miles an hour, and in 1825 built a model locomotive which he placed on a circular railway before his house, Peter Cooper followed with a small experimental engine in 1829 and Miller in Charlestown built a number of locomotives in 1834, but it was William Norris of Philadelphia who in 1836 built the *George Washington*, which resulted in the establishment of the reputation of locomotive builders in the United States. *Austria* [figure 30] is an exhibition model of the 4-2-0 Norris locomotive sent to work in Austria in 1838. The model was built in 1843 by Philip Wolfe, and might well have been used for sales promotion in England, for in 1839-40 the Birmingham and Gloucester Railway had ordered trials for the full-size locomotives upon a severe gradient known as the Lickey incline.

30 (*above*) A contemporary 10-in gauge exhibition model of William Norris's 4-2-0 locomotive and tender, *Austria*, of 1838, built in 1843, by Philip Wolf, the first example of a locomotive with front bogies. 26½ins high by 63ins long.

29 (*left*) A well made 4¾-in gauge model of a typical Bury locomotive and tender, the 2-2-2 *Comet*, with its distinctive turned spokes, circular firebox, haystack boiler and splendid manifold of level test-cocks. 13½ins high by 30½ins long.

The first three engines were the *England*, *Columbia* and *Atlantic*, but it was the *Philadelphia* of 1840 that was the most powerful. This model is probably the first with a 'bogie', and has gab-valve gear and square-section crosshead guide-bars of the same type as the *Rocket*. Another similar model exists, made in 1841, which was given to the Musée du Louvre in 1846, Norris having sent it all over the world, including Japan.

CHAPTER TWO

The Years of Expansion

RAILWAY workings were by now expanding throughout the world. Considering their effects on the economic expansion of every place connected by them, interest in their progress must have been considerable, and yet little evidence remains of miniature railways expressly designed for pleasure before the 1840s. In about 1845, however, E. M. Clarke, an engineer, constructed a 12-in gauge model 2-2-2 locomotive and tender named *Alice* [figure 32]. The chassis and motion details were very similar to contemporary full-size practice, but it was the boiler and tender designs which showed interesting compromises, made for practical reasons. It had a normal steel boiler, but the enormous domes must have been an attempt to get dry steam over a bumpy and possibly temporary or moveable track. The tender was made over-size, with a long well between the frames so that a driver could sit in it. *Alice* was given in about 1858 by Victor Emmanuel II, King of Sardinia, to a railway contractor by the name of Solomon Tredwell, upon completion of a railway he constructed in Italy, but little else is now known of her history.

In 1841 Robert Stephenson patented a new form of valve-gear which consisted of gabs fitted to the top and bottom of the valve-spindle, the eccentric push-rods which engaged in one or other being kept apart by straight links. It was, however, a fitter employed by him called William Howe who developed the current link motion now known as Stephenson's link motion. It is unlikely that either Howe or Stephenson realised its full potentiality

32 A rare photograph of the 12-in gauge 2-2-2 miniature locomotive and tender, *Alice*, built by E. M. Clarke in about 1845, showing the boiler as it was before removal by the Science Museum of London. 40ins high by 74ins long.

31 (*opposite*) The amazing 18¾-in gauge Great Western Railway 2-2-2 locomotive of 1845. It has Jenny-Lind-type solid brass cast dome and rear safety-valve housing. The boiler is mahogany-lagged and carries all the right period fittings. However, it has internal Gooch-type frames, indisputably the valve-gear he designed, and large flangeless driving-wheels. The pressure gauge has been added at a later date. 3ft 7ins high by 9ft 6ins long.

and true usefulness in that it now not only eradicated the wear-prone gabs by substituting for them a much sounder and simpler mechanism, but it also gave, for the first time, a method of 'cut-off' or variable admission of steam into the cylinders, thus saving steam. Robert Stephenson did not patent the new link motion, and soon it was universally adopted. The Great Western Railway had shown themselves to have different views on many aspects of development, and, indeed, in 1845 Daniel Gooch varied the design according to his own ideas. Instead of moving the link up and down from the forward to the reversing eccentric push-rods, he suspended the links and moved the jointed valve-rods, considering that this system further simplified production and cut down moving weights.

Figure 31 is one of the most remarkable models known to the author. Its history is lost. Why and for whom it was made is not known. Although comparatively coarse in design and scale, it has been beautifully made, and must have been the well loved and used possession of some private model railway. Although the funnel-top and tender have been changed, it remains much the same as it must have been when in use over a hundred years ago.

The 1840s saw the production of some of the most famous locomotives. In 1843, C. Beyer, then employed by Messrs Sharp, Brothers and Co. but later of the world-famous Messrs Beyer, Peacock and Co., Manchester, had introduced single iron plates for locomotives frames instead of fletched oak and wrought-iron sandwiched ones. The locomotive superintendent of the Glasgow and Ayr Railway invented the steam band-brake, consisting of a band which could be tightened round a drum on an axle, thus stopping it. In 1846 John Gray produced the famous 'Jenny Lind' class 2-2-2, with his special 'dog leg' valve-gear and outside and inside twin wheel bearings. In that year Gooch, too, was to produce—in thirteen weeks from conception, drawing and pattern-making to machining, fitting and testing—perhaps one of his most famous larger engines, the *Great Western* 2-2-2. In 1841 Robert Stephenson introduced his famous 'long-boiler' locomotives; he continued to produce them till 1847, and, although criticised at

the time, they did result in the general use of steel tubes in boilers instead of copper ones. He had done tests on them for some years because of the economic necessity of ensuring that the resultant longer boiler barrels could be priced the same as the equivalent smaller boilers with copper tubes, but the practice was to continue thereafter.

Stephenson also designed more and more outside cylinder locomotives, such as *Albert* [figure 33], made in 1845 by Alfred Chadburn. That this is a perfect example of the work of an optician is shown in the predominant use of brass, the exotic vine designs cast on the top of the rear dome, the threads used to secure the cylinder-heads which screw on rather like a lens-hood, and the finish, known as 'snailing' or 'curling', produced by rubbing a tam-o-shanta stone lightly over the finished surface, as seen on so many scientific instruments and clocks. Chadburn is known to have made at least two other model steam-engines—a Maudslay table-engine in 1840, and, earlier, a beautiful six-pillar condensing-beam engine in 1829—and the quality in all is absolutely fabulous.

33 A fine $5\frac{1}{2}$-in gauge model of the Sheffield to Rotherham Railway Stephenson 2-4-0 locomotive and tender, *Albert*, built by Alfred Chadburn in 1845, with its outside Stephenson link-motion reversing, fluted funnel and decorated inspection dome. The snailing technique is just visible on the frames, and the threaded cylinder head is typical of opticians' work. 15ins high by 36ins long.

Figure 47 is a contemporary exhibition model of a Stephenson long-boiler 2-2-2 locomotive and tender of 1845. Here, the materials and techniques used indicate that its builder was an engineer rather than an optician. The haystack boiler is riveted steel and the whole model has a remarkable realism and sturdiness about it.

The working model in figure 34 was made by H. C. Ahrbecker of London and, although crude by comparison with the mahogany-lagged 'long-boiler' 2-2-2 model in Paris or the 2-2-2 just mentioned, it was probably built specifically to run on a private model railway in 1845-6. It shows a strong similarity to No. 5 of the Shrewsbury and Chester Railway but bears the number 3 on its chimney front. No. 3 was originally constructed in 1846 as a 2-2-2, but later converted by the Great Western Railway to a 2-4-0 to become almost identical to No. 5.

Perhaps the latest and most successful design of the outside-cylinder Stephenson long-boiler locomotive is illustrated by J. Gardner's beautiful model of the 1846-7 'A' type (2-2)-2-0, built in 1864 for presentation or exhibition purposes [figure 49]. The scale is 1 in to 1 ft and the gauge 6½ ins, which would suggest that the model is of the type supplied to the broad-gauge Holland Eisenbahn, which at that time was laid to 2 metres measured to the centre line of the rails, resulting in 1.95 metres or 6 ft 4½ ins actual gauge. Once again, the general use of brass- and ivory-insulated cock-handles suggests an instrument-maker's work, but oddly enough, upon examination, the easily dropped basket grate shows signs of considerable steaming, despite the lack of wear on bearings and other parts. As with so many such models there was never a tender, but the general workings and inside plate frames are clearly visible, illustrating the design features of the original.

The 1840s also saw the development of the tendency to lower the centre of gravity of locomotives whilst maintaining the higher resultant speeds by enlarging the single driving wheels. Between 1846 and 1848, T. R. Crampton designed his first (2-2)-2-0 locomotive for the Namur and Liège Railway. He claims for his design the advantages of reduced rocking and vibrating motion, which he obtained by lowering the centre of gravity and placing

34 A contemporary 4⅝-in gauge model of the Shrewsbury and Chester Railway 2-4-0 Stephenson long-boiler locomotive No. 3. An interesting feature is the springs, which act on both the coupled driving-wheels which are housed in centrally-pivoted compensating levers. Here too is the first example we see of two feed-pumps driven by their own eccentrics on the driving-axles.

the greater portion of the weight between the supports; an increased heating surface; and an improved arrangement of the working parts, which were externally placed immediately under the eye of the driver. His first locomotive, *Namur*, was completed early in 1847. It was peculiar in as much as the driving-wheels axle was placed behind the firebox, such that the axle extended across the footplate. One leaf-spring acting upon the bearings ran parallel to the axle. On the one hand, the speeds in excess of seventy miles an hour were impressive, but, on the other, such a distribution of weight limited adhesion of the driving wheels, and therefore haulage capacity.

It is perhaps an apt comment on the national characters of France and England that whereas the English preferred a slower, heavier payload, the French were very satisfied with smaller payloads run at break-neck speeds! However, the general outcome was that although the London and North Western Railway ordered a Crampton (No. 200, *London*) with 8-ft driving-wheels, and later the *Liverpool* (2-2-2)-2-0 of 1848, it was the French firm of M. M. Derosne et Cail of Paris who in 1848 took to building them extensively for the Northern Railway of France. Down to the last detail, figure 35 is a perfect model of that type. For many reasons, Crampton locomotives have not been much modelled in this country, and only two are known, though there exist fine examples of such models on the Continent. This is a very good illustration of how people who were then starting to build models privately tended automatically to work on well-loved prototypes. Already the Great Western Railway had attracted more enthusiasts and followers than almost any other railway, with the resultant greater number of models in existence.

Gooch went on to modify his famous *Great Western* and produced his magnificent broad-gauge 'Iron Duke' class 8-ft singles, which ran right up until the end of the broad gauge in 1892. *Hirondelle* [figure 36] is a faithful illustration of its prototype. The model was made by one of the most skilled English commercial builders of the early part of the twentieth century, E. W. Twining whom we shall discuss later.

35 (*top*) A fabulous 8½-in gauge model of the M.M.
Derosne et Cail (2-2)-2-0 Crampton locomotive and tender
No. 122, with its outside cylinders and large
rear driving-wheels as made for the 1851 exhibition. 23ins
high by 79½ins long.

36 (*bottom*) A 7-in gauge model Gooch's (2-2)-2-2 broad-
gauge 'Iron Duke' class 8-ft 'single', *Hirondelle*, of 1848,
built by Twinings in 1927. The main differences between
this and his earlier engine are the roundtop firebox, the
addition of a further pair of wheels in front, and his new
valve-gear.

Tank-engines had been supplied to the Dublin and Kingston Railway by Forrester as early as 1836, and although *Alexandra* [figure 37] is radically different from the 2-2-0 well-tank locomotives of that period, it represents a faithful study of the 1851 2-2-2 tank-engines supplied to that railway. It was made for exhibition work in 1851 by T. H. Goodison of Dublin, and is of a very high standard throughout. Once again an interesting comparison between *Alexandra* and *Colossus* [figure 19], which was built seventeen years before, can be made. There is naturally a hand-brake, but valve-gear and boiler layout have advanced and an attempt has been made to protect the driver by providing a wind-shield, whilst the cylinder arrangement and buffer mechanism remain much the same.

A similar cylinder arrangement is illustrated by the London and North Western Railway 2-2-2 locomotive and tender, *Empress* [figure 38], of which the prototype was built in 1855. Designed by Alexander Allan, these engines were in production from 1845 to 1858, one hundred and fifty-eight in all being built. In 1848, an almost identical engine, which developed a high reputation for speed and hill-climbing, was built by the Vulcan Foundry Company, and was supplied to the Caledonian Railway under the name *No. 15*. The overall very high standard of work was rewarded by numerous medals awarded at exhibitions between 1879 and 1883, but it is interesting to speculate as to why on the one hand he went to the infinite trouble of making a superb selection of scale-size tools and re-railing jacks, and on the other avoided making any springs whatsoever for the engine.

In order to build any working steam model, ideally one should be a good draughtsman, pattern-maker, foundryman, turner, machinist, fitter, boiler-maker, plumber, sheet-metal worker and finally painter. To have so many skills at one's finger tips is rare, and although nowadays there are some people who possess all these attributes, it is hard to find them in early nineteenth-century locomotive-modelling. This can be explained largely by the fact that engineers learned specific skills after arduous and lengthy apprenticeships, and in any case they were comparatively few in

37 A 9½-in gauge model of the Dublin and Kingstown Railway Forrester 2-2-2 tank-engine, *Alexandra*, built by T. H. Goodison of Dublin in 1851. The basic design is virtually the same as *Colossus*. 22½ins high by 46ins long.

38 A fine 7½-in gauge model of the London and North Western Railway Allan 2-2-2 locomotive and tender, *Empress*, of 1855, built by Richard Arkwright at the Crewe works in 1874, with correct boiler, working headlamp, scale-size tools, green upper work and bright red frames. 18ins high by 60ins long.

number. Locomotives themselves were still regarded as highly incredible examples of the latest technical achievement and know-how, and the number of people with the necessary skill and home equipment capable of reproducing these fantastic steam monsters was correspondingly few.

As early as 1815, home workshop equipment was being made for 'the gentleman's workshop' by such people as Holtzapffel, Evans and others, but these gorgeously complicated lathes—capable of turning out anything from billiard balls to highly ornate gothic church towers—were devoted almost exclusively to consuming hours of their zealous owners' time, producing delightfully useless and intricate works of art, the locomotive being regarded as the absolute opposite!

Nowadays, we look upon examples of ornamental turning with a slight feeling of sadness; if all that skill, ingenuity and time had only gone into building the much more artistic and sculptural early locomotives, how much more satisfying would the results of their pains have been.

Only a very few men were engaged in model-locomotive-building as a hobby, and the examples we see are in almost all

cases professionally built and compromised in detail owing to lack of skill and time. This is not to say that there were not enthusiasts; there most certainly were, and objects shaped like locomotives were by now appearing in many guises—silver ink-stands, as in figure 40, tea-making machines, china ornaments, mugs and even 'hot toddy' brewers, a magnificent example of which is shown in figure 39. Possibly of the London and North Western Railway, the beautiful 2-2-2 locomotive, *Glasgow*, was made of silver and represents a locomotive of the 1850–5 period. It is of considerable size and quality, and could well have remedied the ailments of a good ten Scots. The tender contained water and possibly sugar whilst the boiler had a small spirit lamp which heated a generous amount of whisky. This could then be drawn off at the cock on the front over the buffer beam, after it had been pushed along the lairdly table on its silver rails. Interestingly enough, the inside motion is worked by the driving wheels through a two-to-one reduction-gear, giving the impression of fearsome activity as one pushes it to and fro during inebriation.

Locomotives were becoming inevitably larger and more sophisticated and, in order to teach the many students who were engaged

39 (*left*) A superb silver hot-toddy brewer in the form of the 2-2-2 locomotive and tender, *Glasgow*, measuring over two feet in length, from the middle of the 1850s.

40 (*right*) An Austrian ink-stand in silver made in about 1850. The quill fitted in the funnel and the two central domes housed ink-well and sand-sprinkler.

in the study of design techniques, mechanical systems and working principles of building, many demonstration models were made. Companies all over the world specialising in educational equipment, and indeed locomotive works themselves, built sectional, boiler-making and valve-gear models. The 1850s saw the tangible beginnings of attempts to experiment with electrical locomotion. In England a Dr Clarke of Buckinghamshire constructed a $2\frac{7}{8}$-in gauge model of a 2-2-0 electric locomotive, 4 ins high by 7 ins long with a three-pole soft-iron armature geared to large driving wheels. There are twin-coil magnets activated by a crude form of commutator which receives electricity from two little blown-glass Leclanché cells placed over the leading axle. Once again the frames and wheels are brass with the characteristic deep bronze lacquer so often found on machinery of that period. The practice of making sales and exhibition models was now well established and locomotive companies were building or commissioning them as a matter of course for projects all over the world. An interesting example of contemporary work in Egypt is the 2-2-0 well-tank locomotive, *Toussoon Pasha* [figure 41], built by Jeffrey Bey in Alexandria in 1862, the prototype of which worked between Alexandria and Suez. It seems to follow Stephenson practice, in that it is not unlike his last long-boiler design in layout, though of course it is a well-tank and much smaller. Most contemporary locomotives in England still afforded their drivers little or no protection from the elements, and the sun-shade with its arabesque edging gives the little engine endearing quaintness. It is the forerunner of the cab as it was to become.

The 1860s saw the first use of standard gauge on the Great Western Railway and the conversion of engines to suit it. Herein lies a possible explanation of the splendid proportions of the Bristol and Exeter Railway 2-2-2 locomotive model, *Swift* [figure 55], built in 1862 by an engine driver as a reproduction of an engine he had driven. The lowness of the tender and Great Western system of tender brake-gear as found on Gooch engines, together with the size of the boiler, seem almost certainly to suggest that the prototype was a modified broad-gauge. The frame

41 (*above*) A well-made model of the Alexandria and Suez Railway 2-2-0 Egyptian well-tank *Toussoon Pacha* with splendid sun-canopy, built by Jeffrey Bey in Alexandria in 1862. 20ins high by 34ins long.

42 (below) A 4¾-in gauge working model of the standard-gauge Great Western Railway 'Sir Daniel' class 2-2-2 locomotive No. 1114 of 1869, fitted with Stephenson's link-gear reversing. 13ins high by 24¼ins long.

is outside and curves upwards over the driving-axle-box, and there are the typical bracings between all the horn plates. Here again the builder allowed himself a certain degree of artistic fantasy with the curiously-shaped slotting in the polished splashers and the minuscule buffers—quite out of scale with both the model as a whole and such fittings as the carefully executed headlamp. The motion details are excellent and include pumps, Gooch valvegear and well-shaped connecting-rods. Its maker died in 1936, so it is likely that he drove the prototype in his youth and modelled from memory, even though the date, 1862, is painted on the back of the tender.

It should be added that the Exeter and Crediton Railway was opened in 1851 and leased to the Bristol and Exeter. A continuation of this line, known as the North Devon Railway, was opened in 1854 and was worked for some years by Mr Thomas Brassey, a well-known railway contractor. In 1863, both railways virtually became part of the London and South Western Railway and, from being broad-gauge, became standard-gauge lines. Brassey probably used several aged engines which were converted for the standard-gauge usage of the London and South Western Railway.

Figure 42 shows another example of a working model and represents the standard-gauge Great Western Railway 2-2-2 Locomotive No. 1114 of the 'Sir Daniel' class, originated in 1866. The original No. 1114 was one of twenty of that class built in 1869. These engines performed the greater part of the standard-gauge main-line express work for many years, even after the larger and heavier 'Queen' and 'Sir Alexander' classes came out in 1873–5. It is interesting to note that it was not until 1876–7 that makers thought fit to remove the side-sheets and weather-boards and substitute cabs for them—quite long after other major railways in the world had been building cabs on engines. The model is finished in Great Western green.

Between 1859 and 1865, John Ramsbottom designed a class of 2-2-2 locomotives which became known as the 'Ladies'. He believed in light engines throughout his career as chief superintendent, and these popular, powerful little engines did very creditable

45

43 (*left*) A fabulous 9½-in gauge model of the famous London and North Western Railway Ramsbottom 2-2-2 locomotive and tender No. 531, built by H. C. Powell with every prototype detail, including the water-scoop which was fitted to this engine for the first time in the history of locomotive engineering. 2ft 4ins high by 7ft 6ins long.

44 (*right*) A beautiful 3¾-in gauge model of a Great Northern Railway Sturrock *Large Hawthorn* class 2-2-2 'single' of the 1860s, built by a fitter at the Doncaster works with working sand-boxes, scale-size cab fittings and injectors. 10ins high by 19¼ins long.

work. The superb model of No. 531 *Lady of the Lake* [figure 43] is shown as she appeared in about 1873; she has lost the standard green livery prevalent until 1873 on the London and North Western Railway. At this time too, the splasher slots were done away with, and the cab fitted over the side plates. The model was made by H. C. Powell, a professional maker of considerable merit, and is complete and accurate to the extreme. Here also is an engine model that would steam very well and be capable of sustained hard work. The original engines were the first in the world to be fitted with apparatus for scooping up water, while the engine was at speed, out of long troughs lying in the middle of the rails, a system developed by John Ramsbottom.

The 1870s were the decade of the great 'singles', with their enormous driving wheels, slow deliberate beat and classical elegance—a period of transition between the many quaint designs which marked the first half of locomotive engineering history and the ever-growing engines of the latter half.

In mentioning the word 'single' one is reminded of the Great Western Gooch and later Dean singles, the Great Eastern Robert Sinclair singles, and—perhaps the most famous of all—those of the Great Northern Railway.

The forerunner of Patrick Stirling's world-famous express 8-ft 1-in 'singles' was the Sturrock period *Large Hawthorn* 2-2-2 locomotive as rebuilt by Stirling [figure 44]. This model was built to

exceptionally high standards by a fitter of the Great Northern Railway. The motion, with its bearings and beautifully finished detailing, is a complete joy. Paint can easily hide the lack of hours of time-consuming finishing work, but here, wherever the eye falls, fittings, riveting and plate work are without blemish, and paint could only spoil it. Believed to have been made before the turn of the century, this model was last illustrated by Henry Greenly in his 1904 edition of *The Model Locomotive*.

Sturrock had made his name by reintroducing races between railway companies, and by winning with his masterpiece, the famous (2-2)-2-2 inside-cylinder single 215, originally built with a leading 'bogie'. It had been specifically developed to prove to the directors of the Great Northern Railway that it was quite practicable to reach Edinburgh from London in eight hours, stopping only four times en route, and it paved the way to the acknowledged feats of Stirling

It was in 1870 that Stirling produced the first of the 'singles' No. 1, with its 18-in diameter by 28-in stroke outside cylinders, elegant domeless boiler and pierced splashers mounted on the sweeping curve of the running-boards.

Figure 45 is a fine-quality model of No. 1, the original *Flying Scotsman*, completed in 1955 by J. K. Scarth. Although again it is a working passenger model, the springing, riveting and beautiful plate work more than adequately illustrate the superb elegance of

45 A faithful 5-in gauge model of the famous Great Northern Railway Stirling 4-2-2 'single' No. 1, the original *Flying Scotsman* of 1870 built in 1955 by J. K. Scarth with all original details and practical controls for steaming. It includes inside Stephenson's link-motion, axle-driven feed-pump, valve-motion-driven, ratchet-operated, mechanical lubricator and hand feed-pump in the tender. $15\frac{1}{2}$ins high by 57ins long.

the original. In 1879, Werner von Siemens built what was claimed to be the first electric locomotive in the world, which ran on the Berlin Technical Exhibition tracks [figure 46]. Once again a miniature was made, and, judging from the contented expressions on the faces of the passengers, it went very well. It is interesting to note that, even though Siemens claimed that this model was the first electric locomotive, the example mentioned earlier has a much longer authenticated history.

This was not the only example of the building of a miniature

46 A gorgeous party of contented souls aboard the Werner von Siemens 600 mm gauge 0-4-0 electric locomotive at the Berlin Technical Exhibition of 1879.

47 (*opposite*) A well built $7\frac{1}{16}$-in gauge contemporary works model of a Stephenson 2-2-2 long-boiler locomotive of 1845, which was once owned by George Stephenson and is fitted with Stephenson link motion. It has inside cylinders, and, owing to the tendency to flex its frames in motion, it was found necessary to add tie-bars between the exposed inward-looking valve-chests.

railway with the express intention of demonstrating effectiveness of design and the principle of the full-size object. In the early 1860s, Sir R. Macdonald Stephenson, who had already done so much for the development of railways in India, visited China with a view to interesting the Chinese in the principles and economic gains associated with railway construction. Partly because of politics and because his proposed scheme was too ambitious, nothing very much happened, but in 1865 there was talk of forming a company to construct a railway from Shanghai to Woosung, with a jetty and bonded warehouses at Woosung, to which large ocean-going steamers could come, thus simplifying the voyage to Shanghai. After lengthy political struggles and careful acquisition of land, money ran short and it was decided to call a halt to the project.

In 1872, however, Richard C. Rapier conceived the idea of introducing railways to the Emperor of China by constructing a miniature 0-4-0 locomotive and rolling-stock, with the intention of whetting the Chinese appetite. A further advantage of this idea was that the engine was strong enough to take an appreciable load; able to run 15 to 20 miles an hour, and yet was so small that it could be packed up in a case and sent out whole for trial and exhibition in China. In the autumn of 1873 construction began, but it was not finished and tested until the same time the following year. The tests were a great success. In the spring of 1875 the little 22-cwt locomotive was again tried out in front of two directors of the Woosung Road Company, and on one occasion drew eighty passengers at one trip. The boiler provided such an ample supply of steam that the opportunity was taken to increase the cylinder diameter to 5 ins and the gauge from 2 ft to 2 ft 6 ins. It was also furnished with a larger water-tank and appropriately named the *Pioneer*. In October of that year the little train, along with a foreman, chief working engineer, second working engineer, second foreman and general assistant left for China.

Figure 48 shows clearly the construction and the lightness of the engine, as it was lifted on to the track on arrival in China. On 14 February 1876 the *Pioneer* made its first trip, on about three

48 (*opposite*) The first locomotive in China, the little 2-ft 6-in gauge 0-4-0 saddle-tank locomotive, *Pioneer*, built by Richard C. Rapier in 1873-4, being lifted on bamboo poles by Chinese labourers.

Overleaf
49 A beautiful 6½-in gauge Holland Eisenbahn 'A' type Stephenson long boiler (2-2)-2-0 of 1846/7, built in 1864 by J. Gardner to represent the final stage of development of the long boiler series. 13½ins high by 24ins long.
50 A 2⅝-in gauge Stevens' Model Dockyard 4-2-2 tank-locomotive No. 554, *Boadicea*, and truck, of the 1880s. It is a middle-priced model with polished brass boiler, steam-dome, safety-valve, whistle, starting-lever, level test-cock, signal lamp, mahogany buffer beam, twin outside-fixed cylinders with slide-valves controlled by slip-eccentrics, and serrated driving-wheels.
51 A fine 3¾-in gauge Radiguet 2-4-0 locomotive with distinctive Radiguet fittings, crosshead and open-cast frame. 9½ins high by 22½ins long.

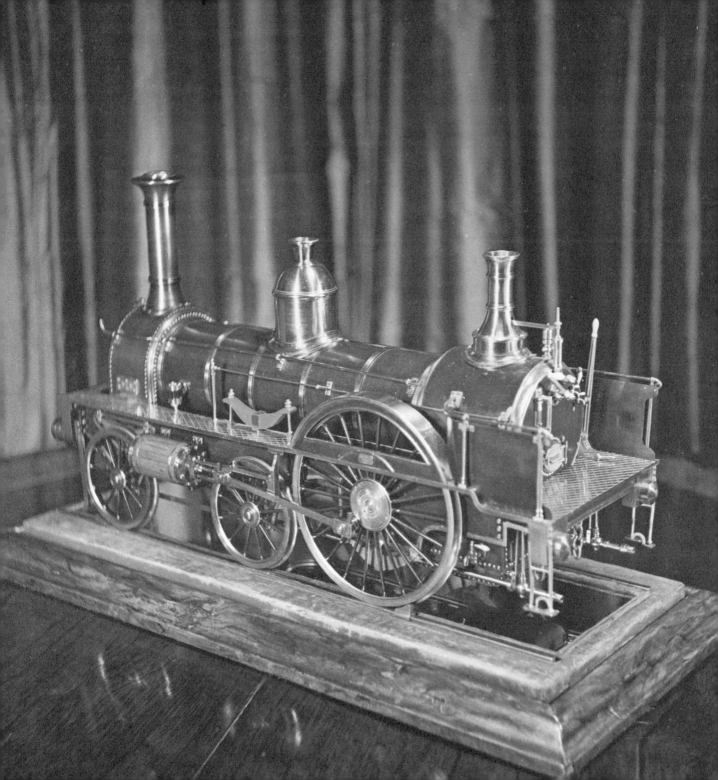

quarters of a mile of rails, to the delight of the Chinese people who flocked to see it at work.

The following quotation is taken from the *Times* of 22 May 1876:

> In the meantime there is no interference with the workmen, who are all country people, and things are progressing rapidly. Several miles of road have been completed and ballasted, and the whole countryside is alive with interest. Literally thousands of people from all the neighbouring towns and villages crowd down every day to watch proceedings, and criticise every item, from the little engine down to the pebbles of the ballast...
>
> The engine, of course, is the great centre of attraction. It is engaged in dragging trucks with pebble ballast at present, and a general cry of 'Laij tze, laij tze!'—'It's coming, it's coming!' heralds each return journey. Then ensues a crowding around and an amount of introspection which suggests awful reflections in case of accident, and then the whistled signal to start; the fall of a live shell could hardly suggest a greater stampede, except that laughter and perfect good temper are present instead of terror.
>
> Everything, therefore, is going on so far satisfactorily; and if the people are let alone by their officials, they will quietly satisfy their curiosity and go home amused and interested. They are giving practical proof at present of what I have always urged—that there is no instinctive dislike in the masses to things foreign. There is only a great deal of ignorance, which can easily be played upon by the officials, and dangerously misdirected if it suits their purpose. Let us hope that this little pioneer railway will get finished without further trouble, and that it will serve to introduce into China a mode of carriage which has done so much to develop the resources of western countries...

From then on gentle expansion continued, not however entirely without incident, for on 3 August an unfortunate lunatic committed suicide on the line, an incident which was graphically reported by the *Times* correspondent, as described, apparently, by a Chinese brakes man on the train.

> My have see one piecey Chinaman. My think e all same belong. Soldier man, he makee walkee on that lailway. All same time my piecey train come that side. Mr Ban-kas makee that engine whistle plenty long time. Then he makee go off lailway litty time. My tink he must wan tshee makee die, caus he makee come that side number two time. My have see that piecey engine hit he. My have all same time puttee on that piecey brake—makee that train stop 'chop chop' (quickly).

In fact the train pulled up in a very few yards and fortunately there were several witnesses who were able to place the question of suicide as a matter beyond dispute. The incident was, however, unfortunate since the Chinese attitude contained an alarming degree of 'an eye for an eye', and it was deemed politic to cease running for a short while. Finally the dispute was settled and negotiations began for the provincial government to buy the completed railway at a price corresponding with its cost, the money to be paid in three half-yearly instalments. The conditions of sale included a clause stating that until the whole amount was paid the company should work the line, not only to gain a year's grace for practical work, but to give China railway experience.

By now larger and more efficient locomotives had arrived and, slowly but surely, administrative and practical problems were beginning to be sorted out. One amusing problem recorded was that the copper coins used by the Chinese were so minute that for some tickets 1,200 had to be painstakingly and laboriously counted out, so that frequently four or five booking clerks were required in the Shanghai office to count the money. To obviate this to some extent tickets were issued so many to the dollar, according to value. Employers soon considered Chinese plate-layers quite equal to English workmen, and as brakesmen and firemen the Chinese were found to be all that could be desired and the trains continued to run steadily and well. From then on the gradual takeover took place without further mishap, and by the spring of 1877 so successful had the exercise proved that it was proposed to pay a visit to the island of Formosa with a view to constructing a railway from one end to the other.

The early development of the railway in China provides one of the best recorded examples of the practical use of miniature railways laid down in the nineteenth century. At this point we will turn our interest to another highly complex facet of model locomotive history—the development of commercially produced toys.

Overleaf
52 One of the first commercial model train sets, the Rotary Railway Express of the 1850s, with its motor and drawing-arm. $1\frac{7}{8}$ins high by 12ins long.
53 A gauge 1 steam Great Eastern Railway 4-4-0 by Märklin, with reversing lever and two-bogie tender.

CHAPTER THREE

Small-scale Commercial Models

EXACTLY when the first commercially-produced toy locomotive models became readily available in considerable numbers is not known. Up until the 1840s individuals could order expensive models for their children, but it was not until the middle of the 1840s that toy locomotives became available to the general public. The reason for this confusion lies in the fact that although some individual companies which became famous after the 1870s proudly state that they were established as early as 1774, no evidence exists of general production before the 1840s.

There exist very few examples produced in the 1850s, but it is interesting to note that even then manufacturers seemed well aware of the romance attached to railway history and based their designs on earlier prototypes which by comparison with the full-size locomotives of that time had an air of quaint antiquity. The Rotary Railway Express [figure 52] is one of the earliest known examples originating from this period, and consists of a little green ¾ in gauge 2-2-2 locomotive and tender and two *Liverpool*-type first-class four-wheel coaches cast in lead and measuring exactly 1 ft in length. The engine, tender and carriages have tinplate floors soldered into position, and the riveting detail on the tender and the hand tooling work on the carriages display an amazingly high standard, given that the whole set complete with its box cost in the region of three shillings. The little train was powered by a clockwork motor soldered into the centre of an attractively shaped and painted lead weight, and a wire arm 18 ins long drew the

54 (*opposite*) A 2⅜-in gauge Stevens' Model Dockyard 2-2-0 'piddler' *Dart*, which boasted an entire length of 6½ins, and was advertised as 'Our Own Make'.

Overleaf
55 A 4⅞-in gauge model of the modified Bristol and Exeter Railway broad-gauge 2-2-2 locomotive and tender No. 1, *Swift*, of 1862, with its splendid proportions and highly ornate pierced brass splashers. 13⅜ins high by 31½ins long
56 Two gauge-1 steam continental Pacifics by Märklin and a gauge-1 steam German 4-4-0 by Bing showing the contrasts in quality and detail. All of around 1910 vintage.

57 A Stevens' Model Dockyard 2-2-0 brass 'piddler' kit of parts which came with boiler, frame, burner, wheels, safety- and regulator-valves, steam pipe, cylinders and axles, mounted on card and ready to fit together, as supplied from the 1870s onwards.

train round in a circle. The instructions on the gorgeously typical period softwood box read as follows:

Having placed the weight containing the mechanism in the centre of a smooth table attach the Engine to the weight by means of the wire, wind up the mechanism and the train will run a distance of about 150 ft, to be considered the first station; detach one of the carriages and it will again proceed about 50 ft (the second station), detach the other carriage, and the Engine and tender will run a considerable distance further making a total of nearly 300 ft.

Even the key, a brass casting, is shaped like a serpent coiled in a figure of eight.

The period between 1850 and 1870 witnessed a rapid expansion in the number of companies that started in earnest to produce working steam locomotive models. In England, probably the most famous company was Stevens' Model Dockyard, which was established in 1843 and continued to produce brass locomotives of many different types up until 1912. Other companies included the Clyde Model Dockyard of Glasgow, established in 1789; Whitney's of London; Newton's of London; The British Modelling and Electrical Company Limited of Leek, Staffordshire; the Leeds Model Company; Lucas and Davies of London; H. Wiles of Manchester; and J. Bateman & Company of London, which was established as early as 1774. In America, Eugene Beggs of New Jersey began to make commercial steam models in the early 1870s, whilst in France and Germany the most famous makers at that period were Radiguet & Massiot, Boulevard Des Filles-Du-Calvaire, Paris and, slightly later, Georges Carette.

As far as can be seen from examining both actual contemporary examples and numerous catalogues there was much swapping, not only of design details but also of names, fittings and even completed locomotives. This is illustrated by the Clyde Model Dockyard and Engine Depot advertisement, reproduced in figure 58 and taken from the back of a very early *Boy's Own Paper*, in which it is clearly stated in the cases of the centre and right-hand illustrations that the locomotives concerned were their new

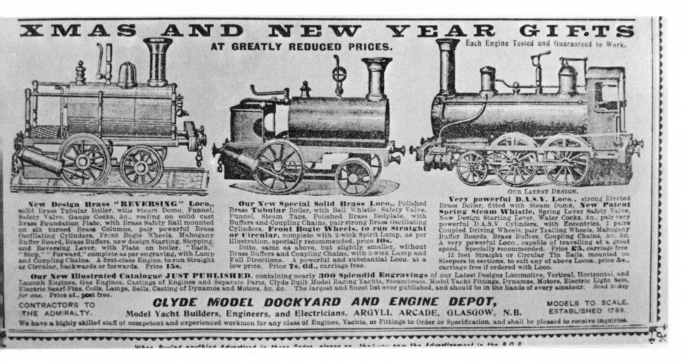

special solid brass ones, of the latest design. In point of fact both these engines were made by Radiguet & Massiot, as is proved by the balls on the tender and frame of the former and the fittings and open-cast frame design of the latter. It is also interesting to note that the advertisement even goes on to mention the 'new patent spring steam whistle' although the wording is carefully ambiguous.

As far as is known, most of these companies started with a few personnel building the little locomotives from standard patterns and selling them one by one. Gradually demand increased so that different designs were produced, and provision was made to supply not only kits for home building (such as that illustrated in figure 57, produced by Stevens' Model Dockyard), but fittings for stationary engines and ship models. By modern standards, of course, they were very small companies and might well have relied upon one another for the supply of generally useable fittings. The standard of the finished locomotives varies a great

58 A Clyde Model Dockyard advertisement taken from an early edition of the *Boy's Own Paper*, blatantly describing Radiguet products as their own. It is amusing to note the wide variety of products in the last paragraph.

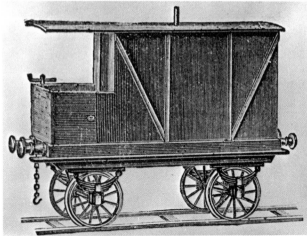

60 (*above*) A Stevens' Model Dockyard polished mahogany and brass Great Eastern Railway truck which was supplied in four sizes.

61 (*right*) A well-proportioned Stevens' Model Dockyard polished mahogany brake-van which was supplied in three sizes.

59 (*opposite*) A gauge-1 electric Gottard 0-4-4-0 locomotive by Märklin of between 1920 and 1925. Again impressive detail and headlamp arrangement.

deal, not only from one company to another but also within the companies themselves. Basically the simplest and cheapest designs, such as *Dart* [figure 54], consisted of a sand-cast brass frame and wheels, brass potboiler with regulator and safety-valve whistle and funnel and twin outside forward-facing oscillating cylinders. These cost a few shillings and later on were finished with japanned and scribed boilers and polished-brass frame tops which were generally band-filed flat on top with coarsely cut chequerwork on the footplates. As the price went up so did the size, the number of fittings and in certain cases the number of wheels, though at this stage there was definitely no attempt to emulate prototype full-size practice. As a breed, in this country they were known as 'Birmingham dribblers' or 'piddlers' owing to the wet trails left behind them on the floor or dining-room table. They must have been fairly dangerous with their spirit firing. In a book proudly named *The Model Steam Engine*, published in 1880, the following instructions were carefully and firmly laid down for running 'piddlers':

DIRECTIONS FOR WORKING MODEL ENGINES

1. To ascertain capacity, fill boiler with cold water, pour whole contents into a measure, and call half this quantity 'a charge'.

62 The best of British 'piddlers' – a 2¾-in gauge 2-2-0 locomotive by Newton and Co. Apart from the beautifully turned steam-dome, safety-valve, whistle, level test-cock and regulator the chassis incorporates an ebony buffer-beam, outside brass plate-frames and twin inside oscillating cylinders which are placed under the footplate, over the burner and exhaust, up the funnel. 7¼ins high by 9ins long.

2. Charge the boiler with boiling water by means of a funnel through the opening provided for that purpose.

3. Where steam-taps are provided, keep them 'turned off' until steam is well up.

4. This will be indicated by a slight escape of steam through the safety-valve.

5. In most model locomotives an upright position of the handle turns the steam on, and a horizontal one turns the steam off. An experiment will settle this point.

6. Whatever the form of engine, after turning on the steam, a few turns should be given with the hand to the fly-wheel or driving-wheel to set in motion, and give time for the heating of the cylinders.

7. Use dry cotton wick for lamps or 'furnaces'.

8. Lamps should not be more than half filled.

9. For fuel, use naphtha, spirit of wine, or methylated spirits.

10. Fill wick-holders with a compact mass of wick.

11. If wick be too loose, spirit rises too rapidly, ignites and overflows.

12. Lubricate all joints freely with feather dipped in olive oil.

13. To avoid injury to furniture, stand models in a tea-tray while working.

Stevens' Model Dockyard produced at least eighteen different designs, which became larger and more elaborate towards the end of the century. Figures 60 and 61 are examples of the quite large range of their rolling-stock, which was in the main polished mahogany with crudely cast wheels, springs, railway and number plates; the range included a wooden brake van, three different wood trucks, carriages, guards/luggage vans, and even twin 'bogie' pullman cars and corridor carriages, which cost nearly twice as much as the others. *Boadicea* [figure 50] is a good example of a middle-range Stevens' Model Dockyard 4-2-2. It is 12 ins long, and is fitted with 'a very strong and safe' polished brass boiler with gunmetal rings shrunk on. One of their finest models [shown in figure 63], is the 4-4-0 tank locomotive number 2538, the *Britannia* early series, 22 ins long and 3⅝ in gauge. All brass locomotives could be run without rails, but tin and wooden rails were available from most companies.

Although Stevens' Model Dockyard were probably the most successful brass locomotive manufacturers in this country, they were by no means the best. For sheer quality of design and finish

probably the best makers of the 1870s were Newton & Company of London; the very fine 2-2-0 locomotive in figure 62 is a good example of their work. Newton & Company produced various other designs, including a 2-2-0 6½ ins long with a single oscillating cylinder again mounted under the footplate, and a slightly larger 2-2-0 with twin outside oscillating cylinders, which was 7½ ins long and 3-in gauge. In both these cases the quality of work is finer and, unlike almost all other 'piddlers', the nearside front bearing has two slots so that the front wheels can be set at an angle when the locomotive is running free.

The British Modelling and Electrical Company, established in 1884, produced a wide variety with common fittings. There are, however, three unique hallmarks which distinguish them—the pierced footplate railings as shown in figure 64, and the positioning of the regulator and the connecting-rod shaping on the 2-2-2 in figure 66. The 2-2-0 in figure 65 was described as a splendid

63 A fine 3⅝-in gauge Stevens' Model Dockyard 4-4-0 tank-engine No.2538, *Britannia*, a more expensive example of the earlier series. It is fitted with a tubular boiler 11ins long, real smoke and fireboxes, internal fire, four coupled driving-wheels 5in in diameter, bogie, Stephenson link-gear reversing, two level test-cocks, bell-top whistle, dome, Ramsbottom safety-valve, cab, three signal-lamps, line-clearers, and four spring-buffers. Later the nameplate was transferred to the tanks, the funnel was shortened, the safety-valve was modernised and the cab shaped to bring it in line with current full-size practice. 10ins high by 19ins long.

bright brass locomotive with cast polished bedplate and side frames, strong polished copper boiler 5 ins long, with starting-lever, water-tap, safety-valve, bell whistle and a pair of very superior oscillating cylinders, all for the price of 14s 6d. Figure 65 is a good example of their mid-priced locomotive, which compared favourably with Newton products, with its turned columns supporting the footplate railings and the added outside frames with their pierced splashers. The boiler was described as a 'bronzed and relieved boiler' with steam-whistle, safety-valve, steam-tap, etc. and particular mention was made of the brass hand-rods along its length.

Figure 66 represents one of their more expensive engines, incorporating as it did fixed cylinders with slip-eccentric reversing, fluted connecting-rods and pierced splashers. The regulator was controlled by a lever in the cab placed as if it were the reversing lever of a full-size locomotive, and the boiler had a firebox with an opening door, and an internal flue with three cross-tubes and proper smokebox. This firm also produced carriages and trucks, but unlike Stevens' Model Dockyard the construction was of sheet brass, japanned and scribed.

Lucas and Davies produced a fairly wide range, and the illustration in figure 67 is of a 2-4-0 which could be supplied in lengths of 18, 24 and 30 ins at prices of £16, £30 and even £60 each, which was very much more expensive than other makers. The reason for the considerable difference in cost was that the boilers had proper fireboxes, tubes and smokeboxes. Full Stephenson link-motion, webbed guide-bars, sprung axles and proper cab controls were also incorporated.

Apart from the work of H. J. Wood, who was an instrument-maker and professional model-builder at the time, the Lucas and Davies locomotives were the most authentic models available. H. J. Wood, the father of the famous conductor, Sir Henry Wood, worked at his premises in London during the latter half of the nineteenth century. The quality of the objects he produced varied enormously, but examples exist of his stationary engines which are among the best ever seen by the author, and it is not surprising

64 A British Modelling and Electrical Company 2-2-0 piddler. The fittings are the same as those used by Stevens' Model Dockyard, but the ornamental sideframes on the footplate are peculiar to this company. 8½ins long.

65 A middle-priced British Modelling and Electrical Company 2-2-0 with pierced splashers, more detailed outside oscillating cylinders, railings and dome.

66 A 3⅞-in gauge British Modelling and Electrical Company expensive 2-2-2 with the characteristic regulator-valve positioning and connection-rod shaping. 15½ins long.

67 A typical Lucas & Davies 2-4-0 as supplied, measuring 18ins, 24ins and 30ins long and costing from £16 to £60.

68 Probably the best available 3¾-in gauge commercially duplicated model of the 1880s to 90s built by H. J. Wood. This is a reasonably accurate Great Northern Railway Stirling 'single' with slip-eccentric reversing, working cylinder drain-cocks and sprung main axle. 9ins high by 35ins long.

that the same man should have produced locomotive models that were probably the most accurate commercial models of their time. He made quite a number of locomotive prototypes, but without doubt the best and most popular one was his Great Northern Railway 4-2-2 Stirling 'single' [figure 68]. This 3¾ in gauge model is accurate enough as far as line is concerned, and incorporates some unusual features. There is a blower worked from the cab and a reverse lever which operates working cylinder drain-cocks. This is possible because the valves are controlled through slip-eccentrics. The axles are sprung, there is a working hand-brake in the tender and a large hand feed-pump is mounted on the left-hand side of the cab outside the frames. Possibly the most interesting feature is the highly successful wagon-type boiler design, which was much easier to build and produced ample steam for the type of work intended.

Like Wood and Newton, Radiguet were primarily instrument-makers to both science and education, but there was a demand for model locomotives and they entered the field. On the whole their engines were more intricate and of better quality than the English and American equivalents, in as much as there was a lot more detail and carefully engineered steel parts. Once again confusion arises in distinguishing the smaller Radiguet engines from those available at the time in England, owing to the common use of certain fittings, but apart from the overall quality there are fortunately clear hallmarks of identification—namely the balls on the cab railings of the 2-2-0 in figure 69, with its typically Radiguet cab-design, their dome shape in the (2-2)-2-0 in figure 70, and the design of their lever-operated whistle. One of the clearest differences in design is emphasised by the fine 2-4-0 locomotive in figure 51 which was built in the 1890s. The connecting-rod is not original, although in outline and shape it is similar to those fitted by Radiguet, but the frames are open-cast, with a thick section on top, and three vertical members and tie-bars connecting them. Although most locomotives of this size were fitted with slip-eccentric reversing, this particular model was fitted with full Stephenson link-gear operated from the cab. The water gauge is a later addition. Other engines of a similar size were produced in a 2-2-2 form with a cab very like the one featured in figure 69,

69 A medium-priced Radiguet 2-2-0 tank-locomotive which measured 300 mm in length and has the typical Radiguet cab and spherical finnials.

70 A Radiguet (2-2)-2-0 Crampton-type locomotive and goods waggon with typical dome and whistle of that company. 300 mm long.

71 (*opposite*) A fine 2½-in gauge 4-2-2 Stirling 'single' No. 776 of 1903 by Carette, with cast-iron front bogie, firebox and tender frames.

and the boilers were almost always japanned and lacquered, with horizontal lines simulating lagging scribed on the surface. Their lengths of rail consisted of delicate interlocking iron castings.

The last stronghold of brass locomotive construction was the factory of Ernst Plank of Nuremberg, but by the time they were discontinued the wheels had become coarse and often set at a pre-determined radius. Also the frames, instead of being cast in brass, were merely bent thin brass sheet.

As far as Europe was concerned the 1890s were to see the beginnings of highly sophisticated scale models built of lithographed tinplate. Nuremberg, with its profusion of skilled cheap labour, was to become the mecca of European activities during the next fifty years.

Märklin Brothers, Georges Carette, Karl Bub, Bing Brothers, Ernst Plank and Jean Schoenner were all prominent companies in this particular sphere, although in the case of Schoenner examples exist of exceedingly complicated, comparatively large-scale models, such as the beautiful 4-4-0 *Luitpold* [figure 72] discussed on page 75.

Theodore Märklin, son of a parson, arrived in the little town of Goppingen in 1840; as a result of the ideas of his wife, Karoline, he started in 1859 to produce children's model cooking equipment for the Christmas market, thus beginning a mechanical and metal toy-making business. On the death of Theodore, Karoline tried to keep the firm going until her three sons grew up, but owing to many difficulties the firm had to be refounded in 1888. In 1891 Märklin were the first to produce sectional tinplate track, and in 1892 their figure-eight formation caused a sensation. It was also the Märklin factory which first used the numerical system of gauges, namely 0, 1, 2, 3 and 4, although there was to be a feud between Bing and Märklin as to the exact dimensions of these gauges (which in any case bore little or no relation to true scale dimensions).

Märklin lasted longer than all the others and produced clockwork, steam and electric models and accessories which were among the best in quality and prototype likeness. They sold engines all

over the world which were marketed by various large stores; figure 53 is typical of one of their middle-priced gauge-1 engines of about 1908. It is, of course, like so many of that period, wildly out of scale, but it was steam, and it worked well, incorporating the interesting twin bogie tender with two wheels on the forward bogie and four on the rear, permitting very tight radii. Figure 56 shows a pair of the famous Märklin gauge-1 continental 'Pacifics', with a Bing 4-4-0 in the background. This provides a good comparison between the two makers, as it illustrates quite clearly the greater amount of detail normally associated with Märklin: the washout-plugs on the boiler fireboxes, the valve-gears and the simulated steam feed-pumps and sanding-domes. Again we find beautiful detail in the gauge-1 Märklin Gottard electric locomotive in figure 59. The factory will probably also be remembered for the profusion of model armoured vehicles produced during the Second World War, which had inside mechanisms to fire caps.

72 An amazing hybrid from the heart of Nuremberg – Jean Schoenner's magnificent 5$\frac{11}{16}$-in gauge model of the Bavarian State Railways BX1 class 4-4-0 locomotive No. 50,000, *Luitpold*, built for exhibition purposes in 1896. The contrast between the amazing amount of superb detail in this model and ordinary tinplate work is a fitting tribute to the versatility of Nuremberg production at the turn of the century. 16$\frac{1}{4}$ins high by 40ins long.

Another difference between the two makers lay in the fact that Märklin locomotives and carriages were hand-painted and lettered over a much greater period and only later were decorated by a lithographic method.

Karl Bub also produced tinplate models of all kinds, but never attained the popularity of Märklin, Bing or Carette, although, like Märklin, their range included armoured toys produced at the same time.

Georges Carette, a Frenchman, migrated to Nuremberg in the 1880s not only because of the work already going on there, but also to take advantage of the low German wages and the skills of the toy- and clock-makers. His range was wide, including, like Bing and Märklin, locomotives in steam, clockwork and electric form, carriages (which were later marketed by Bassett Lowke), stationary engines and accessories. Some maintain that at the peak of his career he attained more accuracy and quality than anybody, and certainly it is true to say that it was a very successful business. For example, one of the important ways in which Carette improved on other makers was in the fineness of the wheel-castings used, a point on which Bing fell down badly. Figure 71 shows a fine example of a Carette 2½ in gauge Great Northern Railway steam 4-2-2 Stirling single No. 776 of 1903, which shows the splendid lamps, clean-cast wheels and castings for the boiler firebox and tender frames. Figure 74 is an unusual Carette gauge-0 2-2-4 steam railway carriage No. 1 with a vertical oscillating engine in the cab and good seating detail in the carriage.

As already mentioned, Ernst Plank produced brass locomotives mainly of the 0-2-2 oscillating-cylinder type, with bent sheet-brass frames. His wheels were coarse in rim-width, and had very large flanges. He also produced varying rolling-stock, but again the wheels were coarse and somewhat whimsically ornate.

The Paris Exhibition of 1900 was important for many of the tinplate producers. It was for this Exhibition that Jean Schoenner built his really fabulous 5¹¹⁄₁₆ in gauge Bavarian State Railways BX1 class express locomotive number 50,000, *Luitpold* [figure 72], which he completed in 1896. It is particularly interesting in as

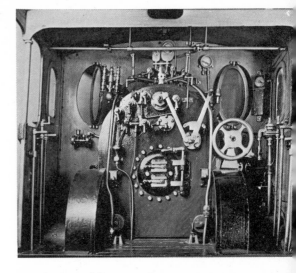

73 The beautifully comprehensive cab detail of *Luitpold*. In the centre is the firehole groove; above it, to the right, the regulator; to the left, the water-level glass and piped level test-cocks. Above the boiler from right to left are the milometer, air vacuum gauge, injector and sanding-dome, steam-valves, pressure gauges and displacement lubricator, and on either side of the cab there are the injector water controls and braking system valves.

Overleaf
74 An interesting little gauge-0 2-2-4 steam carriage No. 1 of 1906-13 by Carette, with its minute vertical oscillating cylinder in the cab.

75 A 2½-in gauge steam 4-4-0 tank engine, *Pilot*, first produced by Bing in 1901-2. Note the standard Bing headlamp which fitted nearly everything in the larger gauges.

much as it shows the tremendous contrasts in the qualities originating from Nuremberg. The wealth of beautifully made, detailed work includes a working Westinghouse pump, top sanding-boxes, scale design injectors, lubricating-boxes with lids on every possible motion joint and guide, lamps, vacuum brakes and reservoir, displacement lubricator, a typical maze of continental pipework and perfect cab details. The Walschaert's valve-gear is an admirable illustration of how meticulously continental engines were designed and built. One can just make out on the valve-spindle-pinion, at the top of the lap and lead-lever, a serrated device enabling it to be rotated and locked in ten different positions, minimising the risk of it becoming oval. The valve chests too, are easily accessible. Underneath the ageing varnish can be seen the original paint of the dark-green cab and splashers, lined in gold and black with deep bronze varnish on the boiler.

It was also as a result of the 1900 Exhibition that Bassett Lowke as a young man first met Stefan Bing and was very highly impressed by continental standards of accuracy. He resolved to persuade Bing to produce models of English prototypes, and the first and most famous of these engines was a 2½ in gauge steam model of the London and North Western Railway 4-4-0 locomotive and tender No. 1902, *Black Prince*. This was on the whole pretty coarse and after modification it became available in 0, 1, 2 and 2½ in gauges in the form illustrated in figure 76. This was one of the most successful designs marketed by Bassett Lowke. He

76 The improved version of the famous Bing London and North Western Railway 4-4-0 *Black Prince* No. 1902. It is a gauge-3 steam version of about 1905.

had visited Bing in company with his great friend and chief designer, Henry Greenly, and as a result the original *Black Prince* was quickly followed in 1901 by a 2½ in gauge 4-4-0 tank engine *Pilot* [figure 75], which had slip-eccentric reversing, and a gauge-2 Midland Railway 4-2-2 'single' No. 54, with third-class carriage and guard's luggage wagons [figure 77]. These were followed by many others, including a 2½ in gauge Midland Railway 0-4-0 tender locomotive No. 2631 [figure 79]; this is a good example of a mid-priced engine of 1903. The Clemencen coach is an interesting alternative design, with its sliding centre bogie controlled by the movement of the front and back bogies, as on continental trams.

Once again Bing Brothers provided ancillary railway equipment and stationary engines and went on to produce in vast quantities for Bassett Lowke. At the outbreak of the First World War, Bassett Lowke concealed the fact that most of his tinplate products were coming from Germany, and in fact the Bing Brothers were expelled from Germany later by Hitler. Figure 78 is one of the more expensive types which, although also a 1903 model, was to set a standard for the products that followed; this particular one is a rare gauge-3 London and South Western Railway 4-4-0 with slip-eccentric reversing and externally-fired boiler; it was common practice for Bing to use the same design for different locomotives, merely changing the colour and number. They seemed to have been particularly fond of the No. 2631, since it appears on many different locomotives in all gauges.

Bassett Lowke themselves were destined to produce relatively few small-gauge models. They often used Bing fittings and scored

77 A gauge-2 steam Midland Railway 'single' and two coaches by Bing which also came out in 1901-2.

78 A fine gauge-3 steam London and South Western Railway 4-4-0 No. 7065, from the Bing stables in 1903. It is fitted with slip-eccentric reversing.

Overleaf
79 A quaintly compromised 2½-in gauge clockwork Midland Railway 0-4-0 and *Clemencen* coach produced by Bing in 1903. Here is a good example of the No. 2631 which appeared on so many Bing models.
80 An English 2⅜-in gauge cast-iron 'push-pull' W. Wallwork and Co. 'Express' 4-4-0 locomotive and six-wheel tender, with their first/third/guards carriages.

81 A gauge-0 electric London and North Eastern Railway 'Mogul' locomotive and tender No. 2848, *Arsenal*, by Bassett Lowke, available from the 1930s.

mainly by producing models even closer to scale, as shown by the 0-gauge electric London and North Eastern Railway 4-6-0 'Mogul' locomotive and tender No. 2848 [figure 81]. Other famous examples were their 'fine-scale' 0-gauge electric *Flying Scotsman* and 'Atlantic' class. It was mainly due to Bassett Lowke in the early 1900s that the model railway was so widely promoted. He had since childhood been interested in trains, and when he took over the family business he was already resolved to produce model railway equipment. He was lucky in having a considerable amount of help from Greenly (whom we shall discuss later), Turner, Twining and a local dairy-owner called Smithies. It was Smithies who designed the water-tube boiler capable of making steam at an adequate temperature and pressure for small locomotives, which had the added advantage of being semi-internal, so that the flame did not blow out. It was not difficult for him to improve on such things as the cast-iron 4-4-0 'Express' tender locomotive and two carriages by Wallwork of about 1890 [figure 80] on the one hand, and the higly elaborate and comparatively expensive limited range of locomotives available from companies such as that of W. Martin of London, on the other. Figure 82 is by W. Martin & Company, a 1901 2-in scale London and South Western Railway Adams 4-4-0 No. 593.

There is no doubt that Bassett Lowke not only possessed tremendous energy but also succeeded in striking almost at every turn the right compromise between the two extremes. In the

early years, virtually the only small-gauge competition in England, apart from other German-supplied retail outlets, was that created by Carson, who produced a series of quite successful small-gauge engines, such as the 0-gauge steam L.N.W.R. 4-6-0 tender locomotive No. 66, *Experiment* [figure 85]. He really preferred larger, more detailed gauges, such as his very fine coal-fired 3½ in gauge Great Western Railway 4-6-2 locomotive and bogie tender No. 111, *The Great Bear* [figure 86]. The model has completely correct cylinders and brake-gear on both engine and tender, while the fine-scale backhead with all its fittings can be removed, exposing practical steaming fittings. Inevitably, the market for such work was limited and the extremely fine castings used for frames on both engine and tender proved an expensive alternative to the tinplate production of the continent. Carson therefore only effectively lasted over a period between 1906 and 1914, despite the very valuable help of J. Crebbin. A medium-priced 2½ in gauge 4-2-2 [figure 87] available from H. Wiles of Manchester, with three-cock water-gauge and slip-eccentric valve gear at eight guineas could not ever have been a serious threat.

Apart from Carson and Wiles, Bonds of London also produced small-gauge equipment, but they tended more towards supplies of castings and material and never really threatened the Bassett Lowke network, which continued to dominate the market until the advent of Hornby. Although this company brought out Meccano in 1901, they did not begin making tinplate train sets until

82 A beautiful 9½-in gauge London and South Western Railway Adams 4-4-0 locomotive and tender No. 593, the castings and drawings for which were supplied at the turn of the century by W. Martin and Co. It measured 2ft 2⅜ins high by an impressive 8ft 10½ins long.

Overleaf
83 Another beautiful American 5-in gauge 4-4-0 locomotive and tender built by W. R. Leudrum of Scranton, Pennsylvania in 1875, which illustrates admirably the typical New World decorations and characteristic outlines. It is fitted with one crosshead-driven feed-pump and the tender has two four-wheel bogies. Note the decorative clack valve case on the side of the boiler-barrel which has a picture insert.

84 The classical elegance of late-nineteenth-century English locomotive engineering, beautifully portrayed by J. McKaig's 4¾-in gauge model of the North Eastern Railway '901' class 2-4-0 locomotive and tender No. 926, designed by Edward Fletcher in 1872 and built in 1883. Fletcher had been apprenticed to George Stephenson and assisted with the *Rocket* at the Rainhill trials. 15ins high by 49ins long.

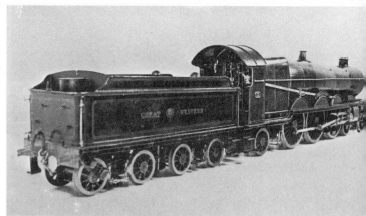

85 (*left*) A typical gauge-1 flash steam London and North Western Railway 4-6-0 locomotive and tender No. 66, *Experiment*, produced by Carson between 1906 and 1913. A distinguishing feature is the cast tender side-frames.

86 (*right*) Carson's 3½-in gauge masterpiece, the Great Western Railway Pacific locomotive and tender No. 111, *The Great Bear*. Note the tender brake-gear details and the fine-scale false boiler backhead. 10½ins high by 53¼ins long.

1915. When in 1923 the British railway companies were grouped into four major systems, Hornby were able to simplify their production into four livery sets and went on to produce comparatively good o-gauge models, such as their successful 4-6-2 *Princess Elizabeth*. Finally, other large companies became involved and Bassett Lowke inevitably began to suffer from having been first in the field.

Contrary to what many people believe, most of the early tinplate trains being sold in the United States in the mid-nineteenth century were not imported from abroad. It did not take manufacturers in America long to realise that there would be considerable demand for miniature replicas of the impressive and exciting trains which by the 1830s were beginning to link up the country and were attracting so much attention. By the late 1830s there were several American firms busily engaged in the production of trackless tin 'push-pull' locomotives and cars, among them the Merriam Manufacturing Company of Durham, Connecticut; Hull & Stafford of Clinton, Connecticut; and Francis, Field & Francis of Philadelphia. Later there were Althof, Bergmann & Company of New York, and James Fallows & Company of Philadelphia. Few of these toys were brandmarked at this early period, Fallows, who used the trademark 'IXL', being one of the exceptions.

The very first self-propelled tin-plate trains to be brought out in the United States were made by George W. Brown & Company, in 1856, and these were clockwork powered; Forestville (Connecticut), where they were made, was then the centre of the clockmaking business in the United States. By the 1860s small gauge commercial production was in full swing, and in 1869, when trans-continental trains first appeared there, the event was reflected in nearly every tinplate factory. In almost all cases these models were designed to be pushed or pulled along the floor and it was only very few and highly expensive models which actually worked by steam, unlike their English counterparts of the period. Nineteenth-century America excelled at producing small, intricate and amazingly accurate cast-iron work. Small cooking utensils, such as an eight-wheel two-second apple-peeler of the 1850s, mechanical toy banks, model carts and trollies all lent themselves to this medium, and it was not surprising that companies started to produce train sets of the push-pull type in cast iron. The first iron engines were made by a company called Ives, and the Baltimore and Ohio 4-4-0 locomotive No. 227 [figure 89] is a typical example of this work. Like the British Wallwork equivalent, the engine was cast in two halves, and was riveted together in two places with neatly interlocking locating lugs. With the iron engines went a variety of cast-iron freight and passenger carriages,

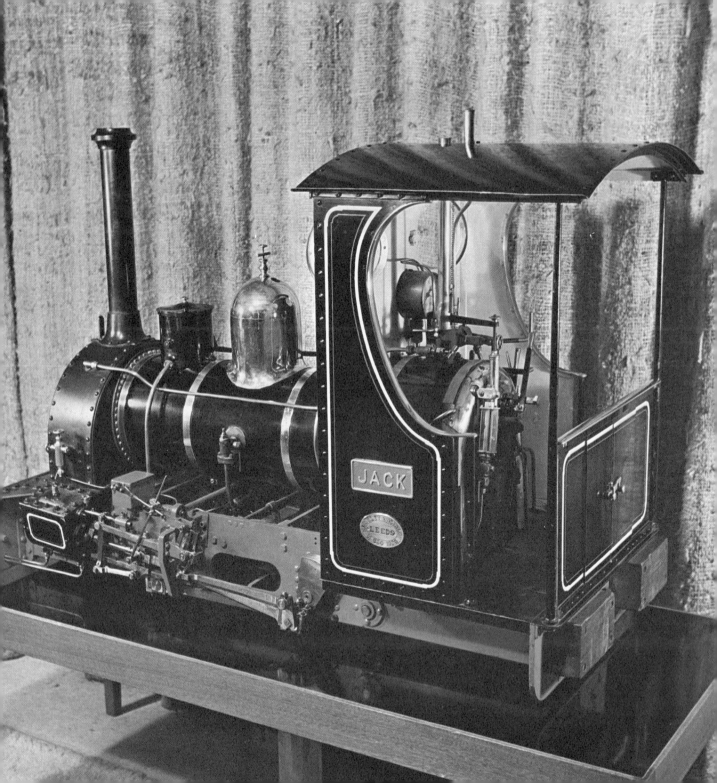

89 A cast-iron Baltimore and Ohio 4-4-0 locomotive and tender No. 227 by Ives.

and frequently both locomotives and carriages were fitted with amazingly detailed figures on the footplates or in the carriages, the most famous of this series being the 999. The Ives Company went on to invent a smoking locomotive which worked with a lighted cigarette, and another containing a cap-firing device.

Perhaps it would be appropriate here to give a brief summary of the Ives Company's history and activities; as Louis H. Hertz says in his famous *Collecting Model Trains* (an indispensable aid to the enthusiastic beginner in this field): 'There can be no question but that Ives trains and what may be said to have become regarded as the Ives legend form a massive cornerstone in any historical interest in or collecting of old model trains.' The business was first established by Edward R. Ives in Plymouth (Connecticut), in 1868, and it was only in 1870 that the Company moved to Bridgeport, Connecticut, the city now associated with the company's name. Their first productions were trackless tin locomotives and trains, and from then on they were to dominate the toy train market until the 1920s—in fact, it is probably true to say that virtually every tinplate train made today in the United States (and in other countries too for that matter) owes something to the pioneering work of Edward Ives and, later, his son Harry C. Ives. By the 1880s and 1890s Ives were making cast-iron trackless push-pull and clockwork locomotives and trains—in this the first in the field, as we have already mentioned—and steam trains

88 (*opposite*) An original 7¼-in gauge narrow-gauge model of the Hunslet 0-4-0 well tank-locomotive No. 684, *Jack*, of 1898, which was especially designed for hauling clay. It was built by R. Marsh in 1967. 24ins high by 37ins long.

manufactured for them by Beggs. At the turn of the century they introduced clockwork track trains into the United States, and ten years later made the first o-gauge electric trains in the country.

The Ives Company did, then, score many important 'firsts', but unfortunately, due to their absolute insistence on quality and their astonishingly generous repair and replacement policy, they gradually ran into financial difficulties, finally going bankrupt in 1928. Control was obtained by a combination of other train manufacturers, and it is this joint ownership which explains the use of certain parts from other manufacturers in the so-called 'transition period' Ives lines of 1928, 1929 and 1930. By 1933, however, the company was absorbed by Lionel of Irvington, New Jersey, and today the only unit on which the 'Ives' name still appears is the 027 track connector.

The stages in the development in America of toy locomotives seems, then, to have been tin push-pull, tin clockwork, live steamers, iron, the first track clockwork trains, the great period of stamped steel, iron and steel, and finally dye-castings. In 1871 Eugene Beggs turned to the production of miniature steam-driven locomotives and was granted his patent, entitled 'Improvement in toy locomotives'. Together with a man by the name of Garlick, Beggs made a variety of steam-driven locomotives which continued well into the early years of the twentieth century. The outlines were generally rather alike, and variety was obtained by modifying wheel arrangements from 4-2-0 to 2-2-0 to 4-2-2 to 4-4-0, and all the engines were fitted with safety-valves behind the cylinders. They were quite expensive, ranging from six to thirty dollars, and an average train with track might well cost in the region of ten dollars.

During the 1870s W. Weeden began building very fine quality model steam-engines, and at the beginning of the 1880s made the 'most perfect and beautiful toy steam-engine possible' for Perry Mason & Company. He then spent over 1,000 dollars on production tooling and by 1884 was in full swing. He began making very many different types of steam engines, tanks and other toys, and in all 10,000 models were to be manufactured. At his death Ritchie took over, but the success of the Weeden engines had been immediate and later a tender and passenger carriage were added, both made out of very thin tinplate with tiny flanges on the wheels. The set became known as the Miniature Railroad. In the 1890s Weeden brought out a second train, apparently of the 4-4-0 type, but eventually (probably owing to the terror of responsible governesses of fire risk), the popularity of other forms of motive power drove him to abandon the production of steam-driven models. At about the same time, Ingersoll Brothers made an unsuccessful attempt to manufacture live tinplate steamers, and the field was left open to the makers of clockwork and electric models.

In America the idea of electric trains was by no means new for, even as early as 1835, a model electric train had been made by Thomas Davenport of Vermont, the inventor of the electric motor. In 1884 a patent on a toy electric railway was granted to Murray Bacon, but the particular train in question was never manufactured, leaving the field clear for Ives, Lionel and Voltamp, who all claimed to have been the first makers of electric models. In any event, the idea caught on fast, and in 1896 Carlisle and Finch began manufacturing the four-wheeled street tram made of polished brass with a simple electric motor geared on to one of the axles [figure 90], mounted on a circular brass strip mahogany sleeper line. It was driven by two Leclanché cells which, according to the recollections of the owner, provided a far from adequate supply. Incidentally, this particular example was purchased in Paris before the turn of the century. The amazing success of this early model precipitated Carlisle and Co. into manufacturing electric train sets, and by Christmas 1897 there were two styles of tram and coal-mining trains on the market. Not very long after this Carlisle & Co. brought out their first electrically-driven steam-type locomotive, the 0-4-0 No. 4. Although it is possible that Carette produced an electric street car in 1893, it is generally accepted that the first electric train sets in Europe were those made by Märklin in 1898, and so it is that America justly claims its lead in the field of miniature electronics. Carlisle & Finch and Howard usually built comparatively light locomotives and carriages with unsprung trucks and few cast-iron parts except wheels, whereas Lionel, Knapp and Voltamp were producing cast-iron frames with working coil-springs. All these makers, with the exception of Lionel, used gauge 2; Lionel favoured $2\frac{7}{8}$ in. The first Lionel locomotive was a model of the Baltimore and Ohio Railroad tunnel locomotive, and was at the time the only electric type in use in America. The Knapp Electric & Novelty Company was founded in 1890, and after years of producing many different toys they finally manufactured electric locomotives in 1906, only to be stopped by competition from Ives in 1913. They were however famous for their 'HO' gauge line.

An amusing development occurred when Howard (producing between 1905 and 1910) introduced a system whereby the tops of carriages could be interchanged, which had immediate appeal for the public, who felt that with just a few carriages they had an immense number of interchangeable parts resulting in a very cheap but wide collection.

By the late 1920s there existed in the United States four major tinplate train manufacturers: Ives, American Flyer, Lionel (destined in the 1930s, as we have seen, to take over Ives), and a comparative newcomer, Dorfan. The Dorfan Company of Newark, New Jersey, was founded in 1924. Good quality 0-gauge clockwork and electric trains were being made by this firm from the outset, and in a year or so a $2\frac{1}{8}$ in gauge was added. For various reasons, Dorfan ceased production in 1936.

There were two particularly interesting American makes of electric trains in the 1920s, both of which, however, were in extremely limited production. The first was the 4-in gauge, three-rail 'Dayton Dinky', which was manufactured by the American Display Company of Dayton, Ohio, in about 1924. A set, which consisted of an 0-4-0 steam type, a flat car and a dump car, track, and controller, was priced at one hundred dollars, a lot of money in those days; it featured both remote control reversing, and remote control uncoupling and dumping.

The second, which was made by the Buffalo Model Company (subsequently renamed the Buffalo Model and Supply Company) in about 1926, was a 2¾ in gauge 4-4-4-4 New York Central Railroad electric-type locomotive. Known as the 'Simplex Electric Locomotive', according to the catalogue it was 19¾ ins long and was powered by two motors. Some collectors have had their doubts as to whether this model was ever actually commercially manufactured, but a photograph of the train has been seen (it was complete with carriages, specified as being 25¾ ins long, and fitted with real glass in the windows), and according to R. Donald Barr, at one time a senior employee of the Buffalo Model Company, some—though indeed very few—locomotives and cars were actually produced.

In Europe, too, the 1920s saw the beginnings of a few new makers, one of the most interesting of which was a company by the name of Edobaud which produced over-scale train sets exclusively for Galeries Lafayette. There were two full sets, one consisting of an enclosed continental electric locomotive and three carriages, including a 'Compagnie Internationale des Petits Express et des Wagons-Lits' electric restaurant car and two others, and the other a flat-back continental electric locomotive with three different forms of truck, one of which had a quantity of drums in it. They have the appearance of gauge-1 equipment and have steel channel frames complete with tie-bars and cross-bracing, interestingly sprung bogies with brass wheels (insulated) and bodywork made of comparatively thick sheet-steel painted and transferred with chromium-plated window frames and opaque cellophane windows. The roofs are pressed aluminium screwed into position, and the trucks have wooden painted bodies. They must have been hideously expensive to produce and inevitably did not last long, production ceasing in about 1932.

A few years later Trix Twin trains set up to make mainly small-gauge die-cast models, and it was not so very long after that and the Second World War that the Japanese entered the fine-scale market, producing very highly detailed HO gauge and o-gauge locomotives modelled on English, Continental and American prototypes (these last included the great 4-8-8-4 articulated American giants).

90 A little all-brass electric 0-4-0 tram by Carlisle and Finch.

CHAPTER FOUR

Large-scale Commercial Models and Miniature Railways

THE period between 1870 and 1910, more than any other, bred men with the time, money and superb capacity for carrying through their fantasies in all fields to a degree inevitably destined to be capped emotionally, economically and socially by the changing standards and shifting fortunes of the war years. This peace and English summer tranquillity is personified by the private railway in figure 91. As early as 1872, Sir Arthur Heywood embarked upon the construction of a 15-in gauge 0-4-0 well-tanked locomotive, *Effie*, which was not unlike the *Pioneer* referred to earlier (p. 51). Apart from his great enthusiasm for railways in general, one of Heywood's justifications for the project was that in his view there was a considerable demand for small locomotives to be used to convey both goods and people across large country estates. In 1874 work started at his home at Duffield Bank in Derbyshire, England, on a most elaborate line, and by the end of 1875, virtually with his own hands, he had completed *Effie*. He soon started work on a second and larger locomotive, with various improvements, which took five years to design and build, and in 1881 both the railway and the new engine were finished. That summer, having published a short descriptive booklet on his views on the railway, an invitation was sent out to the members of the Royal Agricultural Society (which held its annual show that year at Derby), to visit the Duffield Bank Railway. Hundreds of farmers, landowners and estate agents rode in her and although they were impressed—particularly by the new locomotive, *Ella*,

91 (*opposite*) The golden years of private railways. Captain J. A. Holder's wonderful 10¼-in gauge Midland 'single' on the Pitmarston Moor Green Railway at the turn of the century.

a six-coupled engine capable of negotiating curves as small as 25-ft radius and climbing gradients of 1 in 10—no one seemed anxious to invest in Heywood's system and the Duffield Bank railway remained for a long time the only 15-in gauge line in England.

However, he was not discouraged and work continued on the development of locomotives and rolling-stock. Three locomotives were built and a large variety of rolling-stock including parcels van, dining carriage, ballast trucks, wood wagons and open and closed carriages. In 1894, the third locomotive, *Muriel*, an eight-coupled tank locomotive, was completed. Again the line was opened to visitors for three days, and invitations went to engineers, estate managers, quarry owners, public authorities and local dignitaries. Again, a revised booklet was produced and, although virtually no orders resulted, one man, the Honourable Cecil Parker (who was a relative and land agent to the Duke of Westminster) left considerably impressed by what he had seen. He returned to the Duke's estate at Eaton Hall with a view to connecting it with the main-line railway three miles away by just such a system. Soon after this, Heywood was asked to construct a railway at Eaton Hall, which was to be the only other complete railway of his design. This was finished in 1896, but owing to the threat of the motor car his system was doomed, and although he continued to try to promote it, nothing further happened. Both lines carried on running, the Eaton Hall one for work and Heywood's for pleasure—certainly the pleasure element was well understood and recognised by many people at the time. At about that time the narrow-gauge locomotive works of Bagnall built an 18-in gauge model of a Stirling single for Lord Downshire which was used for pleasure, and Savage's of Norfolk had since 1888 been building rather crude little 2-2-0 type locomotives in 18-, 24- and 27-in gauges for amusement parks and fairgrounds.

Bassett Lowke was apprenticed to his father's engineering works during the 1890s, and together with H. Franklin constructed models, displayed them in the store window and advertised in the *Model Engineer* magazine, which was then being run by Percival Marshall, who did much to encourage model locomotive engineering as a hobby. In 1901 he became acquainted with a short, highly energetic and brilliant man by the name of Henry Greenly. They met in their early twenties, at a particular period in English history when there were still large estates, whimsical owners and indeed the possibility of a splendid degree of self-indulgence.

Greenly was born in 1886 and after schooling became apprenticed to jewellers in London. This did not last long and he went back to school and obtained a scholarship to the Polytechnic to study both engineering and architecture. During this time he helped on a fine 18-in gauge Sterling single being constructed by the students from castings supplied by the firm of Bagnalls.

In 1897 he was awarded a first-class certificate for machine-construction and later on in the year was apprenticed to the Metropolitan Railway Company under the General Manager, J. Bell. There he learned to design and drive locomotives, until in 1901 he joined the *Model Engineer*, for whom he started a well-known series of articles. He wrote many articles in the *Engineer* on locomotive design and was a founder of the Society of Model and Experimental Engineers. It was at this time that he met Bassett Lowke. Together they embarked upon what was to be a lifelong friendship, and it was in fact Greenly who designed the *Black Prince* built by Stefan Bing. During this period he was giving extensive talks to clubs, and in 1904 he designed one of the most famous large-gauge engines, namely the 15-in gauge 4-4-2 'Atlantic' locomotive series, the *Little Giant* [figure 92]. This was the first of a series built by Bassett Lowke between 1904 and 1924. It was taken to the Eaton Hall Railway for trials under the direction of A. G. Robins over a distance of three miles during which time it was found to draw a five-ton gross load at a speed of $17\frac{1}{4}$ mph. On the level it could pull 12 tons and when tested at speed 26.4 mph was recorded. Coke was used. Three classes, each bigger than the last, were eventually built and the little giants named and renamed went to private railways and amusement parks all over England. In 1909 Greenly designed the Blakesley Hall 15-in gauge 4-4-4 tank-engine [figure 93], which was the first internal-combustion-engine-driven miniature locomotive.

92 The original 15-in gauge Bassett Lowke
Little Giant. Smaller than the Heywood engine,
it had cylinders 3¾-in bore by 6-in stroke, 18-in
coupled driving-wheels, 9¼-in bogie wheels and
trailing and tender wheels of 11-in diameter.
It had a steel boiler with a working pressure of
110 pounds, and weighed (with its tender) 1½
tons in working condition. It was designed by
Henry Greenly, and is seen here under trial
on the Eaton Hall Railway in 1905 with, left to
right: W. J. Bassett Lowke, his foreman Mr.
Green, Henry Greenly, Sir Henry Leigh, Mr.
Smithie, an apprentice and the Duke of
Westminster's driver.

93 (*opposite top*) Henry Greenly's 15-in gauge
combustion-engine-driven 4-4-4 tank-locomotive
on trial at Blakesley Hall. This was the first of
its type, and was made in 1909.

Greenly continued with the *Model Engineer* until 1909, having already written his book on the model locomotive, but now he edited a magazine with Bassett Lowke called *Model Railways and Locomotives* which continued until its absorption into *Popular Science* in 1923. Perhaps one of the most staggering examples of his energy and versatility is his book of 1907 on flying machines. In 1914 the Eaton Railway witnessed again the trials of his latest design, a 4-6-2 'Pacific', *John Anthony*, built for a racing driver by the name of Captain Howey [figure 94]. It was the only 'Pacific' built by Bassett Lowkes, and when the First World War broke out it went into store until 1915 when it went under the name of *Colossus* to the Ravenglass & Eskdale Railway, where it continued working until it was broken up in 1927.

During the First World War Greenly worked with the Royal Aircraft establishment, where he was known as 'Gunmount Greenly'. When model engineering demands were saturated, he turned to full-size work, but in 1921 he was again designing miniature locomotives, this time the 2-8-2 *River Esk*. *River Irt* [figure 95], with its Heywood valve-gear and interesting circular big-ends, was his modification of the Heywood 0-8-0. This highly

successful little railway was opened in 1875, taken over and re-gauged in 1915 with Greenly as engineer, using for some time rolling-stock and two engines from the Heywood line, *Ella* and *Muriel*, the Heywood 0-4-0 *Katie* [figure 94] from Eaton Hall, a 'Pacific' *Sir Aubrey Brocklebank*, and the *River Esk*. Figure 96 is a typical summer scene.

94 (*bottom*) Henry Greenly's first 15-in gauge 'Pacific' *John Anthony*. It weighed 3 tons, was built by Bassett Lowke in 1913, and is seen here on trial at Eaton Hall in 1914. Captain J. E. P. Howey, for whom it was built, is driving, and Mr. Greenly is in the background. On the left is Sir Arthur Heywood's 0-4-0 locomotive *Katie*, built for the Duke of Westminster.

At the end of 1921, Greenly again contacted Captain Howey and, virtually single-handed, designed one of the most famous and largest model-railway projects ever achieved, namely the Romney, Hythe and Dymchurch Railway. The line was to be 8¼ miles long. He did the surveying, building design and locomotive design, the first of which was the 'Pacific' *Green Goddess*, named after a play currently running in London, and like all the first batch of the Romney, Hythe and Dymchurch engines, built by Davey Paxman [figure 97]. Between 1925 and 1927 seven were delivered (figure 99), and named *Green Goddess*, *Northern Chief*, *Southern Maid*, *Typhoon*, *Hurricane*, *Hercules* and *Samson*, the latter two being 4-8-2s. Later on *Winston Churchill* and *Dr Syn* were built by the Yorkshire Engine Company [figure 98]. It was not until 1925 that he obtained permission from the Southern Railway to go ahead, and it was typical of him that he started work on the station buildings, his own and Howie's bungalows before permission was granted. In 1929, he was again on the move and went back to full-size work, more writing and model design work, until he retired.

Although he did much to promote model railways, Captain Howey was typical of his generation and period and sadly never really gave due credit to Greenly when the railway was finished. Once when he was driving *Green Goddess*, a Southern railway fireman came up to the cab and said, 'Nice little number you've got here mate, wot's the pay like?' to which Howey replied 'Good enough'. Whereupon the fireman said 'Oh really mate, only I

96 (*above*) Period summer scene on the Ravenglass and Eskdale Railway, scenically one of the most attractive in the world.

95 (*left*) Greenly's 15-in gauge 0-8-0 Heywood locomotive rebuild *River Irt*, and a rebuilt *Little Giant*, undergoing trials in 1965 on the Ravenglass and Eskdale Railway.

97 (*above*) A scene in the workshops of Davey Paxman during the construction of no less than five Romney, Hythe and Dymchurch Railway locomotives during the early 1920s.

98 (*right*) The nose of *Dr. Syn*, one of the two Canadian-type 'Pacifics' on the Romney, Hythe and Dymchurch Railway, in 1931.

99 (*below*) An impressive array of Romney, Hythe and Dymchurch Railway locomotives being steamed up ready for a day's work.

100 Recovery work in progress after the sad fatal accident of *Southern Maid* in 1946.

'eard as Howey were a mean old skinflint!' Apart from the odd accident [figure 100], the railway has continued to run successfully since its opening.

Another well known, highly skilful and versatile engineer was E. W. Twining. Apart from being an accomplished painter he was the first in this country to manufacture flying models and designed several full-size gliders and aeroplanes. He started the manufacture of models in 1913, mainly for exhibition purposes. He was also the author of *The Art and Craft of Stained Glass*, *Art in Advertising* and *Heraldry*, but in the field of locomotive models his work will long be remembered for its superb quality and craftsmanship, second to almost none in the period. From then on the field was left largely to people like D. C. Curwen, who produced mainly 10¼ in gauge 'Atlantics' of American outline and 'Pacifics', and Powell, whose work is of exceedingly high quality.

The most important builders on the Continent were the company of Krauss of Munich, who built the little 0-4-0 locomotive, *The Bug* [figure 101], in 1924 for the Romney, Hythe and Dymchurch Railway. It was an adaptation of their standard small tank-

101 The Romney, Hythe and Dymchurch Railway 0-4-0 locomotive and tender, *The Bug*, designed by Roland Martens and built by the Krauss Works at Munich. It is a conversion from a standard industrial tank-engine, the tender being added for the long distance (1926).

102

102 A fine Krauss 4-6-2 'Pacific' locomotive and tender No. 1, at the Munich Exhibition of 1924 during which year Greenly visited the works on behalf of the Romney, Hythe and Dymchurch Railway.

engine and several were made. Their chief designer, Roland Martens, was a great friend of Greenly's and the 'Pacific' in figure 102 is typical of one of their large models. Another company called the Company for Railway Industry, Breslau, built the 2C1 locomotive in the American style to a gauge of 18 ins for a New York amusement park in 1925 [figure 103].

In the United States, the best known large-scale model locomotive builders were without doubt the Cagney Brothers, who started building locomotive models mainly of the American 4-4-0 type at Niagara Falls, New York, as early as 1892. The brothers, Irish by descent, were Timothy (the President), David (the Secretary-Treasurer), Charles and Thomas. Unlike many English and Continental enthusiasts, they were promoters and brokers rather than actual builders of miniature railways, being among the very first businessmen to recognise the fact that train rides through the country's amusement parks would be an extremely popular attraction.

Though they had no monopoly in the field, they were certainly energetic as well as being highly efficient, and as a matter of fact commissioned, over the years, over three thousand locomotives

103 An impressive 18-in gauge American type 2CI class 'Pacific', built in 1925 by the company for Railway Industry, Breslau, for a New York amusement park.

in the narrow gauges. The event which set them on their path was in all probability the breaking of the world speed record in 1893 by the old New York Central and Hudson River Railroad locomotive No. 999. The Cagneys took this prototype and created a miniature live steamer to $\frac{1}{8}$ in scale. Their first products became available in about 1894, some for the $12\frac{5}{8}$ in gauge and some at 15-in. With 999 blazoned on the cab, the only feature missing was the wagon-top at the rear of the boiler; other proportions were in good scale, even down to the 'cowcatcher' and cap stack. All the models, of both gauges, operated well on a level track, but it was soon realised that a more efficient steam generator was needed, as the models had difficulty taking even a slight incline when more than moderately loaded. A larger boiler was devised for them, which more or less solved the problem, though it is probably true to say that the general design of the locomotive suffered because of this modification.

The success of these first locomotives encouraged the brothers to turn to 18-in and 22-in gauge models, but the original 15-in (and the later 22-in) were the most popular and certainly the best looking. They had in fact started with $9\frac{1}{2}$ in gauge but soon abandoned the idea, since their locomotives were primarily designed for fare-paying passen gerloads. Figure 104 shows a typical example on test in Central Park, with their train despatcher, en-

104 A 12⅝-in gauge Cagney 4-4-0 class 'C' locomotive and tender under test in Central Park, New York in 1898. From left to right, the train dispatcher, engineer-in-chief, auditor and general superintendent.

gineer in chief, auditor and general superintendent about to take the engine on a test run. Figure 105 is a Class D of about 1898. They went on to build a variety of industrial 0-4-0 saddle-tank locomotives to various gauges, and in fact offered in their advertising to make any gauge and type of steam locomotive, from 12⅝ in gauge to standard gauge—certainly an ambitious offer, though there are no records of any large-scale engine being built for them.

Several details on these early locomotives mark them indisputably as 'early Cagney'. One rather endearingly comic item on the very first versions of the steam locomotive were the headlights, which were nothing more nor less than the 'carbide' lamps then used on bicycles, though these were soon replaced by more convincing headlights. Another unusual feature of these early engines was the use of hand-rails as lubricating lines from cab to steam chests, but these lacked any support to the boiler, were easily damaged, and, if broken, effectively cut off lubricant to the cylinders.

By 1920 the fame of the Cagney Brothers was world-wide; replicas of No. 999 steamed across amusement parks in Latin America, England, Russia, South Africa and even Japan. But the early 1920s were difficult times, and though the Cagney Brothers tried hard to diversify their products by going into the design of

105 A contemporary photograph of a Cagney 15-in gauge 4-4-0 class 'D' locomotive and tender at Richmond Beach, S.I., with Lake Arbutus in the background during the summer of 1898.

internal combustion engines and gas-engine types (these latter not at all up to the Cagney's usual standard), by 1935 the Company's fortunes had declined to the point of extinction.

A company much like Cagney's was that of Herschell Spillman of North Tonomanda, which from about 1900 produced engines in 15-in and 18-in gauges for amusement park use. Like Cagney's, they favoured the use of castings for the cabsides, thus avoiding, as much as possible, sheet-metal work. Again, their locomotives were mainly of the 4-4-0 type and were in fact rather better than their Cagney equivalents.

In 1915, outstanding work was being done by a single individual, Louis MacDermot, who, rather like Heywood, did a great deal of the work himself. MacDermot proposed internal transport by steam-operated narrow-gauge railway in the grounds of the Panama Pacific International Exposition of that year. There were five locomotives produced in 19-in gauge—an 0-6-0 'switcher' No. 1500 [figure 106], and four 'Pacifics', all of which, including rolling stock, were built in his work-shops at his home in Oakland, California, where he employed about twenty men. The first design, the 0-6-0 switcher, was for use in the construction of the line at the Exposition grounds, with the four 4-6-2 passenger locomotives to follow. MacDermot was determined on exact miniatures for the Exposition, and even the passenger cars were constructed with painstaking care for detail. Of the four 'Pacifics' constructed, only three—Nos. 1912, 1913 and 1914—were actually used at the Exposition; No. 1915 remained in the MacDermot's family estate until his death in 1948.

In 1948 Norman K. Sandley and his father constructed their first locomotive and some coaches and operated a short line in a city park in Janesville, Wisconsin. They were immediately convinced of the feasibility of going into production once again, mainly for amusement parks. Their work is magnificent, and although they produced mainly 'Atlantics' and standard 4-4-0s from 15-in to 36-in gauge, the beautiful 4-6-4 *Riverside* and Great Northern Railway 15-in gauge locomotive No. 4001 [figure 107] is typical of their standard of work. They also produced a fine selection of rolling-stock of all types, running the above railway for testing and promotion purposes.

Perhaps one of the best known and best loved miniature railways in the world, as well as being one of the hardest worked and best maintained, is the Santa Fe and Disneyland Railway. Beginning with an outdoor railway for himself [figure 109] at the Disney estate in Beverly Hills, Mr Disney, who was all his life an ardent rail-roader, expanded his hobby into the bigger operations of the Santa Fe and Disneyland railroad. The 4-4-0s *C. K. Holliday* and *E. P. Ripley* were the first two locomotives to run on the new

106 Shaw and MacDermot's 19-in gauge 0-6-0 'switcher' tank-locomotive No. 1500 in San Francisco.

107 A magnificent 15-in gauge *Riverside* and Great Northern Railway 4-6-4 Sandley locomotive and tender No. 4001.

108 Billy Jones's 19-in gauge locomotive and tender No. 2, *Wild Cat*, with a full train.

36-in gauge railroad with its nine thousand feet of track. The *C. K. Holliday* hauls the freight train and is a southern 'Pacific' type diamond stacker. The *E. P. Ripley*, a cap-stack locomotive, hauls the passenger train. The latest locomotive, the 2-4-4 *Fred Gurley*, which hauls five open cars carrying altogether up to 325 passengers, was originally built in 1894 by the Baldwin Company for a New Orleans plantation owner, and has been completely rebuilt under the direction of Roger Broggie of the Walt Disney Studio's machine shop. These three trains, one freight, one passenger and one excursion, and authentic in every respect, have between them been carrying over one million passengers a year since 1955 when the line was officially opened. Apparently, miniature railways still hold all the attraction for the public that they ever had.

109 The Walt Disney $7\frac{1}{4}$-in gauge standard
4-4-0 locomotive and tender No. 173, *Lilly
Belle*, in steam, at Hollywood.

CHAPTER FIVE

The Concluding Years

By the 1880s more and more people were beginning to model locomotives at home. In 1883 John McKaig completed the magnificent $4\frac{3}{4}$ in gauge model of Edward Fletcher's famous North Eastern Railway 2-4-0 '901' class locomotive and tender No. 926 [figure 84]. It is without doubt one of the best English models of the period, with its immaculate mechanical detail, wonderful scale-size tool-kit and impressive pregrouping livery. This example was at the top of the scale; the other end was catered for by castings and kits which were easily built as supplied by people like W. Martin & Company, H. Wiles and Stevens' Model Dockyard.

Locomotives by now were becoming consistently larger and more complex and provided a greater challenge for model engineers, as is shown by the London North Western Railway 2-4-0 Webb Compound of 1885 [figure 110], the North London Railway 4-4-0 tank locomotive of 1891 [figure 112], and the North Eastern Railway Wilson Worsdell 'rail-crusher' 4-4-0 of 1892 [figure 111].

Through the magazine *Model Engineer*, people such as James C. Crebbin and his son, Roger, were to become well known to readers all over the world for their fantastic collection of 5-in gauge locomotives, *Cosmo Bonsor*, *Aldington*, *Sir Felix Pole*, *Sir James Milne* and *Old Bill*. Another extremely famous name, Dr J. Bradbury Winter, became known for his quite incredibly beautiful 1-in scale model of the London Brighton and South Coast

112 A well engineered $4\frac{3}{4}$-in gauge model of the North London Railway 4-4-0 tank-locomotive No. 14 from the Bow Works of that railway, as designed by Adams in 1868. 13ins high by $31\frac{1}{2}$ins long.

110 (*opposite*) An impressive $9\frac{1}{2}$-in gauge model of the notorious London and North Western Railway 2-4-0 Webb compound locomotive and tender No. 2798, *Marchioness of Stafford*, built in 1885 with working leaf-springs, joy valve-gear and scale-size cab fittings. $26\frac{1}{2}$ins high by 101ins long.

111 (*opposite below*) A fine $3\frac{1}{2}$-in gauge model of Wilson Worsdell's North Eastern Railway 'rail crusher' 4-4-0 locomotive and tender No. 1620, made in 1892 by T. and W. James of the Gateshead locomotive department for Worsdell. 10ins high by $42\frac{1}{2}$ins long.

Railway 0-4-2 locomotive and tender No. 348, *Como*, which represented twenty years of spare-time work and can be regarded as perfection. He also built a magnificent solid silver model of the Rocket to a scale of ¾ in to 1 ft for presentation to the Institute of Mechanical Engineers.

Clubs and private small-gauge garden railways were springing up all over the world, with the accent falling more and more on higher standards and much greater pulling power [figure 113]. Axle-driven feed-pumps on the locomotives and hand feed-pumps in the tenders ensured reliable water supply for boilers on continuous runs. For a long period thousands of working men were able to build an immense variety of cheap, powerful, reliable engines designed by the highly controversial Lillian Lawrence, who wrote for many years under the initials L. B. S. C. Lawrence was a great believer in designs which could be readily made from scrap bits; in all he produced some fifty designs, many of which were modelled again and again all over the world. He believed in power, and as a result many of his designs had over-scale cylinders and boilers which never satisfied the more fastidious model engineers.

Generally speaking, if a locomotive model follows the design of its prototype, apart from fire tube dimensions, and is well engineered, it will prove a successful runner; and as the years passed each new exhibition revealed finer and more powerful engines in

113 Sir Berkeley Sheffield's 4¾-in gauge line in Normandy Park, Lincolnshire with his daughter at the controls of his Great Western Railway *Great Bear*, the first British 'Pacific' locomotive.

114 A magnificent, totally to scale, part sectionalised 9¼-in gauge Mexican Railway 0-6-6-0 Fairlie articulated tank-locomotive No. 41 of 1899, built by the North British Locomotive Company Ltd. Glasgow. The twin box double-ended boiler is complete with stays, double-riveted seams, and all the fittings. 30ins high by 104ins long.

all gauges. Castings for all designs and sizes became available all over the world, and large numbers of the more successful designs were being made.

Throughout this period, professionally-built exhibition and educational models continued to be made. Again the standards were improving, as is evident, for example in the fine quality Fairlie articulated 0-6-6-0 North British Locomotive Company Limited model of 1899 [figure 114], the four-cylinder compound Western Railway of France 4-6-0 locomotive of 1901 [figure 115] and the East Indian Railway goods 2-8-0 locomotive of 1923 [figure 116].

In 1944 the famous and highly powerful War Department 'Austerity' class 2-10-0 locomotives were brought out [figure

115 (*top*) A magnificent sectionalised $5\frac{5}{8}$-in gauge model of the De Glehn-Bousquet type compound 4-6-0 locomotive and tender No. 2702 and 15001 from the company's Batignolles Works in 1901. Again the detail is superb, a worthy tribute to the 'watch building' which went into French twentieth-century locomotive engineering. 17ins high by $67\frac{1}{2}$ins long.

116 (*bottom*) Again, a superb $5\frac{1}{2}$-in gauge model North British Railway Locomotive Company 2-8-0 locomotive and tender No. 1588, built by the locomotive works of the East Indian Railway at Jamalpur, with all the prototype details in scale. $13\frac{1}{2}$ins high by $64\frac{1}{2}$ins long.

117], and locomotives of this size were being modelled all over the world by the few who had the time and facilities to cope with the sheer size and weight of the finished model. Often this meant special pattern-making and castings, and therefore companies produced castings for reliable, powerful little locomotives, such as the 5-in 0-6-0 Kennion *Butch* [figure 119], built by a tool-room engineer by the name of A. Barnes. Tastes, however, vary enormously and one of the most interestingly different recent models is the 5-in gauge narrow-gauge Hunslet 0-4-0 contractors' locomotive model, *Jack*, which was completed recently by Roger Marsh [figure 88].

Size, however, is not necessarily the criterion for impressiveness, as the last three examples show. Figure 118 is a magnificent coal-fired live-steam gauge-1 model of the famous London Midland and Scottish 4-6-0 locomotive and tender No. 6100, *Royal Scot*, built by R. Hines of London. Figure 120 is a fine minute 7¼ in gauge Great Western Railway 0-4-0 tank-engine by H. C.

117 J.N. Liversage's powerful 7¼-in gauge model of the 1000th 2-10-0 war department 'Austerity' class locomotive and tender No. 73755, *Longnoor*. 118 R. Hines' minute coal-fired gauge-1 model of the London, Midland and Scottish Railway 4-6-0 locomotive and tender No. 6100, *Royal Scot*, with its miraculous detail and scale-size working parts.

Powell. Figure 2 is the incredible 7¼ in gauge model of the London Midland and Scottish Railway 4-6-2 locomotive and tender No. 6230, *Duchess of Buccleuch*, which is fitted with four cylinders, twin injectors, working steam sanding-gear, working water-scoop, working vacuum-brakes and couplings, a steam-ejector, full cab details including tip-up seats, sliding roof and windows, and working headlamps with scale-size wicks.

This degree of quality is by no means unique, and as the steam era passes it will be interesting to see whether following generations will turn back to it as a means of exercising their skill and patience. Sadly, time, patience and indeed the requisite skill seem to be less in evidence with the increased pace and pressure of industry, and it is unlikely that this form of self-expression will ever again achieve the same degree of popularity or perfection. So, a fascinating pastime affording the devotee challenge during building, fun and pride on the track and aesthetic pleasure on the shelf, draws inevitably towards its eclipse.

119 A beautifully engineered 5-in gauge 0-6-0 tank-locomotive model, *Butch*, built by A. Barnes in 1964. It is a good example of a fairly simple highly successful freelance commercial design. 12½ins high by 28ins long.

120 A fine 7¼-in gauge model of a Great Western 0-4-0 tank-locomotive No. 1106, built to high standards by H.C. Powell in 1968.

$7\frac{1}{4}$-in gauge model of the London, Midland and Scottish Railway 'Pacific' locomotive and tender No. 6230, *Duchess of Buccleuch*, 21 ins high by 112 ins long (figure 2)

GLOSSARY

Backhead	The back of the boiler with all the steam fittings and driving controls.
Band-brake	A system of braking by tightening a steel band round the perimeter of an axle mounted drum.
Basket grate	A grate with sides such that it could be withdrawn, with its ashes, after a steam demonstration, with minimum mess.
Bed-plate	Solid cast frame.
Bell-cranks	L shaped levers used for transmitting linear motion through an angle.
Cap-stack	An American-type locomotive with a capped chimney for spark cooling.
Clack valve	Non return boiler inlet valve.
Commutator	Rotating electrical contact, supplying current to the twin coil magnets.
Compensating levers	Pivoted levers connected to both axles allowing independent movement born by one point.
Condenser	Apparatus for turning steam back into water.
Condensing beam engine	A beam engine complete with a condenser.
Coupling rod	A rod joining the driving wheels.
Cranked axle	An axle, so bent or cranked, that it can be turned by the push-pull motion of the piston and connecting rod.
Crosshead	The point at which the piston rod is hinged to the connecting rod.
Crosshead guide-bars	Parallel bars maintaining linear movement at the point where the connecting rod and piston rod are hinged.
Cut-off	Point at which steam is either delivered to, or let away from the cylinder, producing, in the latter case, a very staccato beat.
Diamond stacker	An American-type locomotive with a chimney, coned both ways for spark cooling.
Drain-cocks	Small taps at each end of the cylinder which can be opened to allow the escape of any water that forms when the cylinder is cool.
Drawing-arm	Rod connecting the motor to the train pulling it round in a circle.

Eccentric push rods	Controlling rods connecting the eccentrics to the valve spindle through the various differing types of valve gear.
Feed pump	Pump for pushing water into the boiler as it is evaporated.
Finials	Turned decoration on the end of a rod or pediment.
Firebox	The actual section at the back of the boiler containing the grate and burning coals.
Fire-tube boiler	Boiler in which the fire travels to the smokebox and chimney through horizontal tubes in the boiler barrel.
Flash steam	Type of boiler containing a coil of copper tube which rapidly turns the water in it into steam when the flame is played on it.
Gab valve-gear	Two forks on separate controlling rods, arranged such that either one or the other can actuate the valve when it is in any position.
Grasshopper beam	A beam type connection from piston to wheels without central pivot.
Haystack boiler	Boiler with firebox shaped like a 19th – century haystack.
Hotbar-fired	A boiler with a single flue in which is inserted a red-hot close – fitting iron bar which boils the water.
Injector	An apparatus for putting water in the boiler by direct steam pressure.
Joy valve gear	A system of reversing using the linked motion from one eccentric and the main connecting rod through a curved guide.
Knops	Turned decorative bulges in long components.
Lap and lead-lever	A lever giving more accurate timing to the movement of the admission valve in Walshaert's system.
Stephenson's link motion	System of connecting controlling rods and valve, allowing both rods to be controlled by one lever, and intermediate settings which vary the cut-off.
Links	Jointed suspension of connecting bars.
Manifold	A hollow chamber with several outlet points for distribution of steam or water.
Open-cast	A pierced casting.
Oscillating cylinders	Cylinders which are pivoted to remain in line with the stub axles or crank journals.
Parallel Motion	The necessary geometrical linkage to ensure that the piston rod goes up and down in a straight line.
Plateway	Early form of rail, made of webbed cast iron.
Plug-rod	The vertical rod controlling the movement of the plug-valve.
Plug-valve	Semi – rotary conical admission valve.
Pre-grouping livery	The colours belonging to the individual English railway companies before they were combined under the general heading of British Railways in 1922.
Push-rods	The rod connected to both axles allowing independent movement born by one point.
Reach-rod	A rod connecting a cab control to the mechanism operated.

Regulator valve	Throttle.
Return-flue	U shaped boiler fire passage giving increased heating surface.
Rockers	Levers to transmit motion from one moving shaft to another running parallel.
Saddle tank	A locomotive which carries its own water in tanks supported on, or by, the boiler.
Safety valve housing	False decorative case to protect the safety valve.
Sanding domes	Dome shaped sand containers on the top of the boiler, to supply sand for wheel adhesion.
Screw jacks	Jacks with threaded centres which unscrew for jacking purposes.
'Single'	Type of locomotive with only one pair of driving wheels.
Slip-eccentric	Type of valve gear with one eccentric and pushrod, its sheave being able to slip backwards and forwards through 180 degrees against stops on the eccentric, thus altering the timing of the admission valve.
Smokebox	The portion of a boiler connecting the funnel and boiler at the front.
Spring castings	Solid castings shaped to look like leaf springs.
Spurwheels	Toothed wheels.
Stays	Rods holding together boiler plates through the water space to avoid distortion when under pressure.
Steering-tiller	A direct lever for turning the front wheels.
Stroke	Linear distance through which the piston travels.
Switcher	Small American shunting locomotive.
Table engine	A type of stationary steam engine with the cylinder mounted on a table over the crank shaft.
Tender	Wagon pulled behind locomotives, in order to carry the necessary coal and water.
Three-pole soft-iron armature	Soft-iron rotor with three magnetically attracted webs or poles.
2-2-0 type	An engine with a wheel arrangement of 2 front 2 driving, and no trailing wheels.
Water-jacketed firebox	A firebox in which the immediate fire is surrounded by heating surface with water the other side.
Weight shaft	Shaft with counter weights to compensate the weight of the valve motion suspended from them.
Well tank	A type of locomotive, carrying its own water underneath.
Washout-plugs of the water space	Threaded plugs giving access to the inside for cleaning and inspection.
Westinghouse pump	A make of steam air pump for the braking system.